Community Colleges for Democracy:
Aligning Civic and Community
Engagement with Institutional Priorities

Campus Compact is a national coalition of colleges and universities committed to the public purposes of higher education. Campus Compact publications focus on practical strategies for campuses to put civic education and community engagement into action. Please visit https://compact.org for more information

Campus Compact

Community Colleges for Democracy

Aligning Civic and Community Engagement with Institutional Priorities

Edited by
VERDIS L. ROBINSON AND
CLAYTON A. HURD

Foreword by
ANDREW SELIGSOHN

BOSTON, MASSACHUSETTS

Distributed by Stylus Publishing, LLC

COPYRIGHT © 2020 BY
CAMPUS COMPACT

Published by Campus Compact
89 South Street, Suite 103
Boston, MA 02111

All rights reserved. No part of this book may be reprinted or reproduced in any form or by any electronic, mechanical, or other means, now known or her after invented, including photocopying, recording, and information storage and retrieval, without permission in writing from the publisher.

Library of Congress Cataloging-in-Publication-Data

13-digit ISBN: 978-1-945459-25-2 (paperback)

Printed in the United States of America

All first editions printed on acid free paper that meets the American National Standards Institute Z39-48 Standard.

Bulk Purchases

Quantity discounts are available for use in workshops and for staff development.

Call   1-800-232-0223

First Edition, 2020

CONTENTS

FOREWORD   X
Andrew J. Seligsohn

INTRODUCTION   1
Advancing Institutional Priorities through Civic and Community Engagement
Verdis L. Robinson

1. CIVIC LEARNING AND ENGAGEMENT AT COMMUNITY COLLEGES   12
   Institutional Characteristics and Practices of Community Engaged Campuses
   John Saltmarsh
   Glenn Gabbard

2. BLENDING CIVIC AND CAREER EDUCATION IN THE "IN-BETWEEN" SPACES   37
   The Minneapolis College Example
   Lena Jones

3. CIVIC AND COMMUNITY ENGAGEMENT AFTER THE SUMMER OF HATE   50
   Connie Jorgensen

4. CIVIC ASSESSMENT AT DELTA COLLEGE   58
   Measuring Change in Political Interest, Civic Attitudes, and Likelihood of Future Participation
   Lisa Lawrason

5. FORGING GUIDED PATHWAYS FOR CIVIC AND POLITICAL ENGAGEMENT   71
   Developing a Partnership to Provide Civic Opportunities for Students That Span Their Enrollment at Two- and Four-Year Institutions
   Sarah J. Diel-Hunt
   Stephen K. Hunt

6. DEMOCRACY'S COLLEGES REVISITED 85
Creating an Inter-Segmental Civic Engagement Pathway between California Community Colleges and the California State Universities
   Patricia D. Robinson

7. CHANGE OF PERSPECTIVE 104
Finding your Community Engagement Fit to Put Students First
   Erin Riney

8. DEVELOPING AND ASSESSING HIGH-IMPACT, CLASSROOM-INTEGRATED SERVICE-LEARNING PROJECTS 116
   Lori Moog
   Emilie Stander

9. PUBLIC ACHIEVEMENT 131
Increasing Student Persistence and Completion through Robust Political Experiences
   John J. Theis

10. THE ARC OF ASSESSMENT LEADS TO STUDENT SUCCESS AND SOCIAL AND ENVIRONMENTAL JUSTICE 142
Kapiʻolani's Service and Sustainability Learning Program
   Robert Franco
   Krista Hiser
   Francisco Acoba

AFTERWORD 156
   Brian Murphy

EDITORS AND CONTRIBUTORS 159

FOREWORD

The decisions we make about education are decisions about the kind of country we want to be. That is true, most obviously, in the context of decisions about whom we educate--that is, whether it be only the rich or everyone, only males or everyone, or only the dominant ethnic group or everyone. But it is equally true in the decisions we make about the ends for which we educate students. Do we educate them to be members of a ruling class? Do we educate them to be citizens among equals? Do we educate them to be captains of industry? Do we educate them to be obedient workers?

In many nations, these questions are answered explicitly in national policy. In the United States, however, they are resolved through a combination of secondary effects of apparently unrelated policies and decisions made by states, localities, and individual institutions. There is no national test, for example, that determines who will be educated for the professions and who for the trades, as there is in many countries. Instead, all pathways are, in principle, open to all students.

But the realities of economic inequality, educational inequity at primary and secondary levels, health disparities, housing and employment discrimination, and a host of other factors, structure the genuine opportunities open to actually-existing students. And because all of these factors are, in the United States, themselves filtered through the foundational reality of systemic racism, we end up with an educational opportunity structure shot through with class and racial hierarchy.

In this context, the task of giving meaning to the ideal of equal opportunity falls, in higher education, to America's community colleges. These institutions are the door that opens the widest for students from low-income communities and communities of color. Community colleges are the places where families that have never experienced the opportunity for higher education can change the dynamics of inter-generational wealth and poverty.

Against that backdrop, efforts in the last decade to strengthen community colleges have been welcome. Initiatives designed to ensure that community colleges are giving students the best chance at success mean that the promise of college as an engine of opportunity can be realized by an increasing proportion of community college students. The fact that those efforts are increasingly characterized by attention to the specific barriers facing students of color is also a welcome development

It is hard to miss, though, that these efforts at improving community college student success have proceeded on the basis of a specific vision of the kind of education community college students need. The student is assumed to be a person whose primary need is for a credential that will enable them to earn a middle class wage. In light of the economic realities faced by community college students, it is undoubtedly important that colleges provide students a pathway to financial stability for themselves and their families. However, if that is as far as a community college education goes, it will fall short of meeting the demands of democracy and of justice.

The policies and practices that create the economic and racial inequality facing so many community college students will not be changed by helping some of them make it into the middle class. Those policies and practices will change when people who are affected by them can mobilize the political and financial power necessary for re-shaping the public agenda.

Community colleges must provide their students with an education that enables them to claim their public voice at the local and national level. That is what students at selective four-year institutions expect from their college educations; we should expect no less for community college students. In fact, in a world where low-income students and students of color depend on community colleges, the education offered by those institutions is the education that will either destabilize or reinforce the injustice in our economy and our democracy.

Campus Compact views higher education through our commitment to full participation communities and a full participation America. We believe every person has an equal and legitimate claim to play an active role in shaping the economic and political lives of the communities of which they are a part. We expect colleges and universities to provide educational opportunities consistent with that aspiration.

For community colleges, this means marrying the effort to open up economic opportunities for students with an equally-robust effort to open up opportunities for participation and voice in the political process. We offer this collection of essays in that spirit.

Andrew J. Seligsohn
President, Campus Compact

Introduction

THE DEMOCRATIC COMMITMENT OF COMMUNITY COLLEGES

Advancing Institutional Priorities through Civic and Community Engagement

Verdis L. Robinson
Commmunity College Civic Engagement Specialist

The notion of community colleges as "Democracy's Colleges" is a very common one in the community college civic engagement world. It echoes back to the 1947 Truman Commission Report on Higher Education for Democracy which argued for the creation of a nation-wide system of community colleges. Since then, community colleges, as local institutions, have become an essential part of the American landscape of higher education, playing key roles to democratize it and to provide more people access to the "American Dream." With an emphasis on affordability, accessibility, and open-access admission practices, community colleges have secured higher enrollments of lower-income, non-traditional students and students of color as well as a high percentage of immigrants and English-as-a-second-language students.

However, community colleges face unique challenges. One is the difficulty of sustaining a holistic campus life for students given that most are commuter schools whose students spend the majority of their time in the community working, taking care of families, and engaging in other responsibilities outside of their classes and off campus. Additionally, the dominant four-year college assessment model for student success, as well as a prevalent misconception of community colleges as simply "junior colleges," has tended to make community colleges virtually invisible when compared to their four-year public and private sister colleges and universities. This invisibility is particularly unfortunate given the access to higher education that community colleges provide as the embodiment of a democratic society.

How then, to make the invisible more visible? How do we get more to take notice of the wealth and worth of community colleges? How do we take back the regard of community colleges as democracy's colleges, and their students, in turn, as democracy's agents? To that end, how do we ensure that community college students graduate as civically engaged, informed, and active agents of change? How do we make civic engagement and learning a priority in community colleges for the future of our democracy?

Community colleges are especially well positioned to harness the need and desire to provide benefit for the larger communities in which they are placed and, at the same time, deepen the educational experience of their students. However, with decreasing budgets and, in many cases, decreasing enrollments, we are seeing priorities scaled back to only those that would appear most obvious in their ability to advance institutional success and effectiveness. In this context, continued support for civic engagement programming and activities has languished considerably or, in some cases, disappeared altogether. Unfortunately, student civic engagement remains among the most least understood effective strategy to advance such institutional and student success goals, particularly given what many would regard as its impact assessment challenges.

This leads us to the key question of this book: How do we show that, in fact, civic engagement and learning strategies can be leveraged in very powerful ways to advance priorities related to institutional effectiveness, college completion, and student success? A begin to answer that question, a brief overview of the major efforts to date is warranted.

Community College National Center for Community Engagement

Founded in 1990, the Campus Compact Center for Community Colleges (later named Campus Compact National Center for Community Colleges) was established to help community colleges deepen student engagement through community service. Its mission was to serve as a national advocate for community colleges in service-learning and civic engagement in an effort to sustain the work as a national movement. Additionally, the Center served member institutions in the promotion and implementation of community service as a means to improve teaching and learning for the benefit of students and the communities in which they live.

By 2003, the Center was renamed the Community College National Center for Community Engagement (CCNCCE) and hosted by Mesa Community College. In the 25 years of its existence, CCNCCE disseminated service-learning funds through grants to US community colleges in order to help them develop and enhance their service-learning and civic engagement programs. The Center created generate a network of community college educators who incorporated service-learning and civic engagement across a variety of academic disciplines, becoming role models for other educators to emulate. This networking was achieved through an annual conference that provided opportunities for community college faculty, staff, and administrators to learn from each other's programs and make service-learning and community engagement a central part of community college students' experience at their respective institutions (Conss, 2001, p. i).

Additionally, the Center furthered its mission through publishing an on-line journal, *The Journal for Civic Commitment*, supported by the federal government's Corporation for National Service. Published biannually, the journal was dedicated to growing and strengthening the discussion and research agenda around service-learning and civic engagement in community colleges. The Center closed its doors in light of its host institution's shifting administrative and financial landscape, based on "careful evaluation of changes in its priorities and fiscal realities."

The Knowledge Net (2000)

In April 1998, the *American Association of Community Colleges* and the *Association of Community College Trustees*, supported by the W. K. Kellogg Foundation, launched a joint project to offer a comprehensive vision for the future of community colleges. They called it the *New Expeditions* initiative, and launched with it a coordinating committee that would commission research papers, public hearings, focus groups, and community-level conversations nationally. The result of the year-long effort was a report entitled "The Knowledge Net" (National

Association of Community Colleges, 2000) which aimed to establish a strategic direction for community colleges, challenging them with a series of recommendations for action. The 50-page document explored community college connections to learners, the campus itself, and to the community. For learner connections (which the commission intentionally preferred to "student" connections), the report recommended a shift in focus from the act of "teaching" to the embracing of "learning" as a means of forging a pathway to greater access, equity, and inclusivity. It recommended repackaging courses, policies, and schedules to "meet the needs of lifelong learners as customers" (p. 17). In the area it called college or campus connections, the report suggested that "all members of the college community must be partners for student success…as the institution's highest priority" (p. 23). This includes a positive and professional work environment for a diverse and competent faculty. It also recommended that "community colleges prepare more people for higher education leadership roles and strive for more diversity in all leadership positions (p. 24). Furthermore, it stated that "identifying and preparing more women, and people from underrepresented groups, to fill community college presidencies and upper-level administrative slots is essential" (p. 25). To these ends, it was recommended that community colleges model equity and democratic practices and leadership.

In its recommendations related to community connections, the report specifically emphasized the civic role of community colleges. In fact, the report began by stating, "A democracy depends on people knowing how they connect to their community, state, and nation" (p. 3). Among its particular recommendations were that "community colleges should use their widespread community prominence and accessibility to help forge positive relations among diverse segments of society" (p. 4). It suggested community colleges become places that the community at large trusts as a neutral space to build common ground and emphasized the need of colleges to develop local leaderships through the building civic skills for a "functioning democracy," in addition to occupational skills (p. 5). Furthermore, in regard to workforce development, the report offered the following telling recommendation: "Community colleges should view basic literacy, English-as-a-second-language, and remedial programs as essential parts of their mission with positive effects on democracy and economic life" (p. 8).

So, twenty years ago, a key strategic direction for community colleges in the 21st century involved owning their civic role and leadership. At the same time, community colleges were emboldened not only to facilitate communication and learning, but also to lead "the changes needed for true, life-long learning in a world driven for technology and a global economy" (p. 35). This later statement, in fact, was the report's primary challenge to community colleges. Yet, twenty years since the report's publication, the work of civic engagement and democratic learning are again perceived as largely distinct and separate efforts, apart from these broader institutional goals, with little acknowledgment or realization of the potential interconnectedness of this work with institutional priorities such as workforce/economic development, completion/pathways, access/equity/inclusion, and assessment/accreditation.

Community Colleges Broadening Horizons through Service-learning Program

Between 1994 and 2012, the American Association of Community Colleges worked with 104 community colleges through its Community Colleges Broadening Horizons through Service-learning program. The effort was funded through the Learn and Serve America program, a government program under the authority of the Corporation for National and Community Service that provided opportunities for students nationwide to participate in service-learning projects and gain valuable experience while helping communities. According to its report,

> The Horizons colleges placed a total of 32,000 service-learning students in community-based organizations and K-12 schools. The students provided 496,000 hours of direct community service (a monetary value of $10.8 million, according to Independent Sector, a leadership network for nonprofits and foundations); worked with 2,400 community college faculty; and affected more than 5,300 local agencies and schools and 600,000 individuals" (Prentice, Robinson, & Patton, 2012, p. 6).

As service-learning was being used by faculty in many community colleges, and student involvement was found to relate to gains in civic, academic, workplace, and personal benefits, the Horizons study investigated the possible connection between participation in service-learning and student retention. Leaders believed that if the program could show how service-learning fostered gains in retention and persistence, it would provide administrators who were seeking attrition interventions through already-existing programs on campus a proven tool to promote student success. While limited by student differences in the number of attrition risk factors, findings indicated that such a connection may exist through the increase in retention-positive factors in service learners.

The Horizon's study concluded with the encouraging claim that the use of service-learning has a "prism effect," claiming that "a single semester of service-learning produces multiple student outcomes, even when the instructor does not have additional outcomes in mind when integrating service-learning into his or her course" and that "discovering one intervention that provides community college students—as well as the community—with this multitude of benefits can only be helpful in meeting student needs more efficiently and effectively" (p. 26). The findings showed that educating for democracy, particularly for community college students, can create the space where students can be challenged and changed, an essential learning condition given the understanding that "student success lies not only in academic gains, but also in personal, social, and civic development" (p. 26).

The Democracy Commitment (TDC)

Despite what currently appears to be a growing de-emphasis on civic and democratic learning as key strategies for success in community colleges, not all institutions have abandoned ship. In 2011 and as a reaction to the crisis of democracy and ongoing sense of urgency over the public's lack of confidence in our political system (a moment that would be outlined in the National Task Force on Civic Learning and Democratic Engagement influential publication *A Crucible Moment*, 2012), a group of community college representatives came together to form The Democracy Commitment (TDC), an initiative committed to "reclaiming their colleges' democratic mission and responding to this time of crisis" (Ronan, 2012, para. 2)

The founders, Dr. Brian Murphy (see afterword) and Dr. Bernie Ronan, stated in the inaugural declaration of TDC that:

> American higher education has a long history of service to democracy. Our nation's colleges and universities have always had a mission to make education available to the many and not only the few, to ensure that the benefits and obligations of education were a democratic opportunity. This is a proud history, but it is not enough. Beyond access to education itself, colleges and universities have an obligation to educate about democracy, to engage students in both an understanding of civic institutions and the practical experience of acting in the public arena. The American community colleges share this mission of educating about democracy, not least because we are the gateway to higher education for millions who might

not otherwise get a post-secondary education. More critically, we are rooted deeply in local communities who badly need the civic leadership and practical democratic capacity of our students for their own political and social health." (quoted in Ronan, para. 5).

The organization provided a platform for the development and expansion of community college programs, projects, and curricula that aimed to engage students in civic learning and democratic practice across the country. Its goal was that every student of a US community college graduate with an education in democracy, and it rallied to achieve that goal while rejecting "the deficit model so prevalent in the national narrative about [community college] students" (Murphy, 2014, p. 23).

TDC insisted that a commitment to expanding the democratic capacity of community college students "requires institutional intentionality and public conversation about this dimension of the work" (p. 23). Furthermore, it must be part of institutions' mission and strategic planning, and part of institutional life.

During its 2011-2018 tenure, and housed in the Association of American State Colleges and Universities (AASCU), the TDC partnered with such organizations and initiatives as AASCU's American Democracy Project, the Association of American Colleges and Universities (AAC&U), Fair Elections Center, Kettering Foundation, NASPA Lead Initiative, and Community Learning Partnerships (CLP) to provide its national network of community colleges with programing, projects, trainings, and annual convenings in order to fulfill its mission and goals.

Community Colleges for Democracy (CC4D)

In 2018, TDC merged with Campus Compact, a national coalition of 1,000+ colleges and universities committed to the public purposes of higher education. With this merger, Campus Compact created a new network for its 240 community colleges, *Community Colleges for Democracy*, which signifies a national commitment to community colleges, to civic engagement, and to democracy. The national network of community college members committed to preparing students to be informed, active, and mobilized leaders in their communities, states, and the world, in addition to preparing them for the workforce, careers, and continued education.

Given the fact that community colleges enroll nearly half of all students and play a disproportionate role in educating students from communities that face exclusion as well as first generation students from all backgrounds, community colleges are central to Campus Compact's mission of ensuring that higher education contributes to the health and strength of our democracy. Preparing students for democracy and preparing them for the workforce, careers, and continued education are mutually reinforcing. Naming and framing the work already being accomplished at community colleges as civic learning and democratic engagement is essential to its advancement as well as making it a priority. As Campus Compact engages higher education in the effort to achieve full participation in our communities, our democracy, and our economy, community colleges must and will stand front and center.

CC4D provides a framework for connecting with community college professionals to share approaches that are effective in linking community-based civic learning to broader goals for retention, completion, and education for democratic participation. One key strategy has been through offering national and regional communities of practice (CoPs) specifically for community college professionals, providing training and resources for faculty and staff working to maximize community and campus assets to achieve shared goals. Beyond these efforts, CC4D continues to offer a wide variety of professional development opportunities for faculty, staff, and administrators through state, regional, and national conferences and events. Campus Compact remains committed to serve as the national megaphone to raise awareness about the public purposes of community colleges and raise the profile of community colleges as central to the role of higher education in building democracy.

Organization of The Book

This book argues that in order to fulfill the public purposes and the original mission of community colleges, the intentional prioritization of civic learning and democratic engagement is necessary. The chapters provide evidence of strategies and innovative ways that community college campuses have extended their efforts to institutionalize civic learning and democratic engagement and the impact of those efforts. Collectively, the case studies that follow suggest that to ensure civic engagement and democratic learning for all community college students, community college leaders should intentionally *align* and *infuse* civic engagement and democratic learning with their institutional priorities, making their connections apparent and measurable. In other words, there are a variety of effective strategies to educate community college students for democracy while advancing student and institutional success.

As the chapters in this book will attest, there are many examples of these alignments and infusions which have been successful in both sustaining civic engagement efforts on community college campuses and positively impacting the college's relationship to community as well as students' experience with community engagement and leadership. A strong case will be made in this volume that use of civic engagement and democratic learning programs, initiatives, and pedagogies like deliberative dialogues, service-learning, community-based learning, electoral engagement, and student organizing/leadership training need not, and in fact should not, be segregated from the efforts to advance institutional priorities. By separating them, in fact, our commitment to the public purposes of higher education will never be realized.

This book offers ten chapters that illustrate various levels of institutionalization of civic learning and democratic engagement and the ways in which they are aligned with strategic priorities.

The first chapter shows how campuses have made civic engagement a complement to (rather than a replacement of) their workforce readiness missions through the lens of the Carnegie Elective Classification for Community Engagement. Chapter two provides a case study on blending civic education with career education at Minneapolis College, detailing the successes and the challenges that civic advocates and educators have experienced.

The third chapter provides a rich case study where, in response to events that deeply impacted the community of Charlottesville, Virginia, Piedmont Virginia Community College made civic engagement an institutional priority. The essay details strategies that were used to integrate civic issues and engagement into the curriculum. The fourth chapter, from Delta College in Michigan, looks at the integration of civic learning into the curriculum as well and introduces effective strategies to measure change, motivation, and likelihood of future civic participation based on students involvement in civic engagement learning and leadership.

Chapter five provides a case study detailing a unique partnership between Heartland Community College and Illinois State University that is designed to build an academic civic pathway that forges the development of civic skills from the community college to the university. This pathway aligns completion and transfer priorities with civic skill building and education. In a similar vein, Chapter six details a project which is building an inter-segmental civic engagement pathway between community colleges in California and their four-year feeder schools, working within the framework of the Guided Pathways model.

The seventh chapter brings us to North Carolina where Durham Technical Community College has revised their community engagement efforts to address the unique challenges and opportunities of their community college students. Similarly, Chapter eight explores how Raritan Valley Community College in New Jersey reviewed and redesigned their service-learning curricula to foster an institutional culture committed to engagement in meaningful civic actions.

In chapter nine, Lone Star College in Texas aligns robust political experiences for students with student persistence and completion priorities, utilizing the youth civic and community engagement model, Public Achievement. Kapi'olani Community College in Hawaii presents an evaluation model of assessing civic ethos in community colleges in Chapter ten, expanding it to include sustainability priorities as well.

Conclusion

Community colleges, because of their many close ties to their communities, are indeed "community's colleges" both in principle and in practice, and therefore are uniquely positioned to support students to become civic leaders at home and globally (Zlotkowski *et al.*, p. 19). While helping student achieve their highest academic potential will always be a top priority of community colleges, as Schnee, Better, and Cummings (2016) have eloquently stated, "our most important civic engagement work is to help our students learn to imagine not just a better future for themselves, but a more just and equitable world in which they desire, and are prepared, to be engaged citizens" (p. 6). It is to empower, to remove barriers of opportunity politically, economically, and socially that inhibit and prohibit full participation in our democracy through political and non-politically processes for our students and in the communities from which they live and *with* which our campuses serve. The road to greater justice and equity does indeed runs through community colleges.

References

American Association of Community Colleges and the Association of Community College Trustees (2000). The Knowledge Net: A Report of The New Expeditions Initiative. Washington D.C.: Community College Press.

Conss, Lyvier. (2011). In J. F Swaba, (Ed.). *Beacons of Vision, Hope, and Action* (p. i). Mesa, AZ: Community College National Center for Community Engagement.

Murphy, B. (2014). Civic Learning in Community Colleges. In J. N. Reich (Ed.), *Civic Engagement, Civic Development, and Higher Education: New Perspectives in Transformational Learning* (pp. 19-24). Washington, DC: Bringing Theory to Practice.

Prentice, M., Robinson, G., & Patton, M. (2012). *Cultivating Community Beyond the Classroom*. Washington, DC: American Association of Community Colleges.

Ronan, B. (2012). Community Colleges and the Work of Democracy. *Connections: The Kettering Foundation's Annual Newsletter*, 31-33.

Schnee, E., Better, A., & Clark Cummings, M. (Eds.). (2016). *Civic Engagement Pedagogy in the Community College: Theory and Practice*. New York City: Springer International Publishing.

Zlotkowski, E., Duffy, D. K., Franco, R., Gelman, S. B., Horvell, K. H., Meeropol, J., & James, S. (Eds.). (2004). *The Community's Colleges: Indicators of Engagement at Two-year Institutions*. Providence, RI: Campus Compact.

Chapter 1

CIVIC LEARNING AND ENGAGEMENT AT COMMUNITY COLLEGES

Institutional Characteristics and Practices of Community Engaged Campuses

John Saltmarsh
University of Massachusetts, Boston

Glenn Gabbard
New England Resource Center for Higher Education

Community colleges originated with the democratizing role of opening access to higher education and were complemented by a mission that included civic preparation, or what the founding statement of *The Democracy Commitment* has called "democratizing opportunity and doing the work of democracy." Over time, community colleges have reshaped their institutional identities to serve multiple purposes and missions, some of which are in tension with each other. These include institutional emphases on academic transfer and vocational training. These functions are part of long-held historical commitment within the community college movement to community responsiveness, primarily through the assessment of long- and short-term labor market needs.

Research is needed to better understand how community colleges are fulfilling their historical role as "democracy's colleges" in ways that broaden a focus on access, completion, and transfer while acknowledging their commitment to respond to economic imperatives, so that community colleges can effectively act as institutional citizens and prepare students with the knowledge, skills, and values to be active participants in a diverse democracy (Zlotkowski, et.al., 2004).

This study, conducted as part of a research initiative of the Kettering Foundation exploring practices in civic learning and democratic engagement at community colleges, is guided by the following primary research questions:

1. How do community colleges express their democratic mission, including their historical identity as "people's colleges"?
2. How are community colleges operationalizing their civic mission?
3. What are the distinctive assets and challenges of community colleges in fulfilling their civic mission?

After analyzing findings from the study, we offer a number of recommendations of how community colleges can deepen their efforts to develop the civic agency of their students and strengthen their roles in the democratic life of their communities. These recommendations, we hope, can serve to productively inform institutional decision making and planning for community colleges looking to harness civic learning in order to advance a range of institutional priorities, including student success and workforce development.

Methods

One way to explore how community colleges are fulfilling the role of "democracy colleges" is to examine campuses that have demonstrated a commitment to and claimed an organizational identity defined by community engagement. This study examines the campuses that have received the Elective Community Engagement Classification from the Carnegie Foundation for the Advancement of Teaching. The campuses receiving this classification actively sought the status by submitting evidence through an extensive application process. The Carnegie Foundation defines community engagement in this way: "Community Engagement describes the collaboration between institutions of higher education and their larger communities (local, regional/state, national, global) for the mutually beneficial exchange of knowledge and resources in a context of partnership and reciprocity." In applying for the classification, campuses provide evidence in the areas of institutional culture and commitment, curricular engagement, and outreach and partnerships."

The sample for this study consists of seventeen community colleges that have received the classification through three classification cycles: five campuses in 2006, six campuses in 2008, and six campuses in 2010. Across the three classification cycles, seventeen community colleges were classified, and 294 four-year campuses were classified. The seventeen campuses also represent variation across the Basic Classification provided by the Carnegie Foundation (Table 1.1).

Table 1.1 Community Colleges with the Elective Community Engagement Classification by Basic Classification (2006, 2008, 2010)

2	Assoc/Pub-R-M: Associate's—Public Rural-serving Medium
3	Assoc/Pub-R-L: Associate's—Public Rural-serving Large
3	Assoc/Pub-S-SC: Associate's—Public Suburban-serving Single Campus
3	Assoc/Pub-S-MC: Associate's—Public Suburban-serving Multicampus
1	Assoc/Pub-U-SC: Associate's—Public Urban-serving Single Campus
4	Assoc/Pub-U-MC: Associate's—Public Urban-serving Multicampus
1	Assoc/Pub2in4: Associate's—Public 2-year colleges under 4-year universities

In this exploratory study, we conducted a textual analysis of the applications looking for distinguishing characteristics, patterns of data, and key indicators that provided evidence of civic practices. We undertook a descriptive analysis of the data to provide findings and to interpret the meaning of the findings.

Research Significance

Through a study on characteristics of community engagement at community colleges using the Carnegie data, it is possible to 1) get a better understanding of how community engagement is being implemented at community colleges and, by focusing attention on what it means to be a democracy college, identify indicators/criteria for what constitutes a democracy college; and 2) provide guidance to community colleges that seek to advance a more explicit civic mission regardless of whether they intend to seek the Carnegie Community Engagement Classification.

Limitations

A limitation of this research is that the number of campuses—seventeen—is small and perhaps not representative of the community college sector as a whole. Across the United States, there are 1,655 community colleges (Digest of Education Statistics, 2001, Table 244). Roughly 1 percent of the total number of community colleges in the United States is represented in this study. The small number of community colleges that have participated in the Elective Community Engagement classification may be due to the pervasiveness in the sector of under-resourced institutional environments. Assembling the data for the application requires a commitment of staff and faculty and administrative resources that may not be available at many community colleges. Because of the small number of campuses analyzed, statistical analysis is not useful. Additionally, prevalence data is not useful in understanding community engagement on the sample campuses. Also, the data reported in the applications is self-reported, and with that brings the limitation that it is not verified, and its accuracy has not been corroborated. Additionally, the applications provide evidence for community engagement activity but not the quality of that activity.

The structure of the Carnegie Community Engagement Classification application is such that it seeks to gather information about "what" the campus has done regarding community engagement. It does not seek information as to "why" campuses undertake community engagement. While there are questions on presidential leader statements and strategic planning that sometimes reveal something about the rationale of the activity, for the most part this data is not available through the applications. Further research seeking to better understand the motivations for campuses undertaking community engagement could be done through qualitative research using interviews of campus leaders of engaged campuses to better understand the institutional motivations for engagement.

Further research on community engagement at community colleges should be conducted using the 2015 classification data when it becomes available. Also, the Carnegie Applications could be analyzed in conjunction with the data from the Community College Student Survey of Engagement (CCSSE). It is apparent from this study that many of the campuses use the CCSSE to assess the impact of their community engagement activities on students.

Findings

The applications from the Carnegie Community Engagement Classification indicate that 1) community-engaged community colleges specifically articulate a "civic" mission; 2) executive leadership shapes a vision of community engagement in which community engagement and economic imperatives are complementary instead of being oppositional and, thus, strategic planning and institutional priorities are shaped in ways that advance community engagement; 3) the civic mission is primarily operationalized through the curriculum through service-learning, and thus community engagement is defined as the work of the faculty – and, as core faculty work is embedded in the curriculum, resources are devoted to faculty development, and community engagement is valued in the hiring, review, and promotion of faculty; and, 4) to implement a strategic priority of community engagement, engaged community colleges have developed infrastructure to support it.

Claiming a Civic Mission

Fundamental to being a community-engaged campus is a guiding mission and vision that articulates and shapes civic efforts. All of the applications provide evidence of a civic mission. The civic mission is a part of what is typically articulated as a multifaceted mission: access, student success, workforce development, lifelong learning, and responsible citizenship.

Representative examples from the applications follow:

> "[X Community College] is a premier learning community whose students and graduates are among the best-prepared citizens and workers of the world."

> "To promote Civic Engagement and Leadership is one of the six active college-wide goals. . . . Objectives under the goal include; fostering civic leadership among students, supporting service-learning courses."

> "Although the current mission statement does not mention community engagement . . . The Board of Trustees . . . have mandated that each student will have completed at least one service-learning/civic engagement designated course before approval for graduation."

> "We are a student and community-centered institution fully engaged in the life of the community and a vital resource enabling student development and success as well as civic and economic growth and development."

Leadership

Executive leadership appears to be essential in shaping the civic mission and priorities of the campus. This is expressed most often in the vision the president sets for the campus and in the strategic planning and assessment documents of the campus. Leadership relates to the mission in the sense that academic leaders are shaping campus missions to enact a vision of community colleges that educate students for engagement in a diverse democracy.

Representative examples from the applications follow:

> President: "it is important to remember that the end result of the learning experience here is an informed, enlightened, and productive citizen as well as a productive worker."

> President: "By combining classroom instruction with a service activity, students gain real-world life experiences, as well as sense of civic responsibility."

> Strategic Plan: "[the goal is to] transition [X Community College's] service-learning function – expanding into new courses and disciplines with a focus on those underrepresented – as one of several areas within an overall applied learning organization."

> Institutional Impacts: "From a number of sources, such as annual reports, budget narratives, interviews, newsletters, service-learning and civic engagement activities increase the institutional profile of the College. A key finding is the College's revision of its mission statement to include 'service' as part of its goals of education for citizenship. This has led to tying service to institutional and accreditation goals and created a campus and community-wide understanding of civic engagement for students, faculty, community partners. It has helped the college review and redesign curricular and develop an institutional culture that is committed to community engagement."

Operationalizing the Mission in the Curriculum

The applications indicate that at the core of an identity as an engaged community college is the institutionalization of service-learning in credit-bearing courses through a pedagogical method to achieve civic engagement. This goal gets expressed in mission, strategic planning, infrastructure, resource allocation, faculty development, curriculum, instruction hiring, and rewards. Service-learning as a curricular strategy functions as the primary means of implementing civic engagement as part of a community college education.

As a president was quoted in one of the applications: "So the challenge is how do we teach good citizenship. One way that [X Community College] reinforces and reaffirms this life plan for students is through our service-learning program." Ultimately, as a teaching institution with high teaching loads and predominantly contingent faculty, an academic priority such as civic engagement has to become the work of the faculty and be embedded in the curriculum if it is to be successful. As a strategy for advancing the goal of student engagement, civic engagement has to be in the curriculum because students who come to community colleges participate primarily in the curriculum, not the co-curriculum.

Representative examples from the applications follow:

Learning Outcomes: "College-wide Competence is . . . social and civic responsibility. . . . We have adopted a general education competency stressing the importance of civic engagement. This call for students to demonstrate the importance of caring for one's self and the awareness of civic and cultural issues relevant to the past, present, and future."

Learning Outcomes: "Service-learning is an integral part of the College ReVisioning movement and affords avenues for students to meet Success Skills requirements that are critical to the new vision. . . ."

Faculty development: "support to attend national and regional conferences, workshops on topics such as reflection, syllabus development, program design in collaboration with community partners, and integrating civic responsibility into the curriculum."

Faculty Hiring: "[X Community College] uses a rubric for hiring faculty using selection criteria that specifically addresses expertise in and commitment to community."

Faculty Hiring: "The college has not made community engagement a requirement in hiring faculty. However, . . . faculty are making it known that service-learning and community engagement is expected as a learning pedagogy, thus creating a teaching culture among faculty members, which is influenced within the hiring of new faculty members."

Faculty rewards: ". . . There are no promotion and tenure policies in place. It is apparent to the campus community, though, that faculty who are committed to civic engagement and the integration of meaningful service-learning experiences as integral parts of their courses are the faculty who emerge as leaders in their departments."

Faculty rewards: "Teaching effectiveness—faculty who integrate service-learning into their curriculum can provide course materials . . . to document how the use of engaged learning practices can positively impact student learning outcomes. "Scholarly/professional growth—Many . . . faculty who use service-learning in their courses are able to document their research and attendance and presentations at national conferences specifically targeted to the scholarship of community engagement."

Faculty rewards: "When evaluating a staff member for promotion, scholarship of community engagement is considered. When providing faculty members with continuance of contract during the first three years (per union), implantation of service-learning or civic engagement is considered."

Coordinating Infrastructure

Each of the classified campuses, in line with their mission and strategic priorities, has devoted resources to a structure on campus to support civic engagement, or more specifically, to support service-learning pedagogy as practiced by faculty and quality service-learning opportunities in the curriculum for students. The Carnegie Classification uses the language of a "coordinating infrastructure" asking the questions: "Does the institution have a campus-wide coordinating infrastructure (center, office, etc.) to support and advance community engagement?" The infrastructure includes staff and budget designed to support faculty professional development, community partnerships, and student learning. The coordinating infrastructure, as an academic support unit, typically has a reporting line to academic affairs. The evidence from one application was typical in discussing the mission of a campus structure: "The mission . . . is to provide service-learning training for faculty and staff and opportunities for students. . . . to integrate service-learning into the technical and general curricula . . ." Other expressions of coordinating infrastructure from the applications include the following:

[Coordinating infrastructure]:

"serves as a catalyst to expand and enhance learning for students and promote democratic values of citizenship, service and civic engagement.

"seeks to build sustainable partnerships to match the learning needs of the college with the needs of the community."

"supports all service-learning initiatives. Develops community partnerships and many volunteer experiences."

"to provide service-learning training for faculty and staff and opportunities for students."

Analysis

Democracy's Colleges

It appears from the data in the applications for the Carnegie Elective Community Engagement Classification that the community colleges that received the classification have clearly and intentionally identified and advanced a civic mission. While there is language in the applications about "civic engagement," "community engagement," and "social responsibility" as an institutional goal and as an outcome for students, these are not well defined or conceptualized in ways that would guide implementation, program development, curricular design, or assessment. The most common articulation of civic purpose and practice is through "service-learning," which is specifically supported through resources and structures, through faculty development, and through policies and incentives.

In the Carnegie Community Engagement Classification, "community engagement" has a specific definition: "Community engagement describes the collaboration between institutions of higher education and their larger communities (local, regional/state, national, global) for the mutually beneficial exchange of knowledge and resources in a context of partnership and reciprocity." The term "civic" is the most common framing in the applications and may resonate more strongly, ironically perhaps, with community colleges than "community" because of their public function.

It also may be that an emphasis on the "civic" may serve as a counterweight, or as a complement, to pressures to account for workforce development and completion outcomes. As one campus noted, "our goal is that, through our institutional endorsement of civic engagement, we are helping to mold better, more engaged citizens." Civic engagement is a complement to, rather than a replacement of the workforce mission: one campus stated that it was meeting the goal of preparing the "best-prepared citizens and workers" through "a range of applied learning programs and activities." A President is quoted that "the end result of the learning experience here is an informed, enlightened, and productive citizen as well as a productive worker." One strategic planning document stated that "we emphasize not just intellectual and workforce development, but civic engagement as well . . ." and that the college "prepares our students for additional study, for entry into the workforce, and for engaged citizenship."

These colleges seem to be taking an approach of explicitly claiming a civic mission as well as embracing their access and completion mission and their workforce mission. All of these missions are essential and are related to each other. As a Community College Survey of Student Engagement report notes, "The higher a person's educational attainment, the more likely he or she is to be gainfully employed, pay taxes, volunteer, participate in the democratic process, and be able to take care of the health and educational needs of his or her children" (Center for Community College Student Engagement, 2010, p. 3).

Embracing multiple missions in a way that integrates civic with other purposes may be the hallmark of what it means to be a "democracy college." Civic is framed as a compliment, rather than an alternative, to other mission imperatives. It is the core framework in the founding declaration of "The Democracy Commitment":

> Beyond access to education itself, colleges and universities have an obligation to educate about democracy, to engage students in both an understanding of civic institutions and the practical experience of acting in the public arena. The American community colleges share this mission of educating about democracy, not least because we are the gateway to higher education for millions who might not otherwise get a post-secondary education. More critically, we are rooted deeply in local communities who badly need the civic leadership and practical democratic capacity of our students for their own political and social health.

The Carnegie applications suggest that engaged community colleges are explicit in articulating a mission and purpose that recognizes their historical and social complexities while implementing public engagement practices that are intended to fulfill the democratic role and civic purpose of the community colleges. Analysis of the applications indicates that engaged community colleges express a civic institutional identity through their mandate, mission, and practice (Table 1.2).

The evidence from the classification applications suggests that engaged community colleges function as "democracy's colleges" in so far as they manifest and integrate a democratizing public mandate, a civic mission, and intentional public engagement practices operationalized in the curriculum. In this framing, the classified community colleges are revitalizing the democratizing function of the community college by moving beyond an access function, and moving beyond an economic opportunity function, to a civic ethos function. This is expressed in way that claims that access and opportunity are essential but not sufficient.

Table 1.2 Institutional Identity and Outcomes of Democracy Colleges

Institutional Identity	Outcomes
Democratizing Role (mandate)	Social mobility Access Opportunity
Civic function (mission)	Preparation for life, work, and civic participation
Public Engagement that operationalizes the mandate and mission (practice)	A. Understanding civic institutions B. Practical experience with activity in the public arena (service-learning)

At the same time, there is little evidence in the applications that Community Colleges, in advancing a civic mission, are intentionally connecting access, opportunity, and civic priorities with the institutional priority of student retention and success and with the institutional priority of diversity and inclusion (in regards to students, faculty, and staff) (Strum, et. al, 2011). This might be an area for further study and attention.

Service-learning and Civic Engagement

The campuses in the study all implement service-learning as both a pedagogical and curricular strategy for advancing a civic engagement mission. Given the context of students who have complex life, work, and family commitments and financial challenges, a focused academic strategy seems appropriate. "Community college students typically are a multitasking group," writes McClenney, "juggling their studies with work and family. Often, they also bring an array of family, academic, or other challenges with them to college. Consistent with these realities, a strong and recurrent theme in findings from the CCSSE survey is that community college students are far more likely to be engaged in their learning within the classroom than outside of the classroom" (2007, p. 143). Service-learning is a curricular approach that changes classroom practice in a context where "moving the needle on student outcomes at community colleges substantially depends on what happens in the classroom. College must make the most of the time students spend with their instructors" (Center for Community College Student Engagement, 2010, p. 8). Ultimately, at a teaching institution with high teaching loads for predominantly contingent faculty, an academic priority such as civic engagement will have to become the work of the faculty and be embedded in the curriculum if it is to be successful.

While campuses undertake multiple programs intended to, as the applications reported, "create a campus-wide culture of engagement"—"through curriculum, co-curricular activity, community outreach, and service-learning," or through "fostering civic leadership among students, supporting service-learning courses, participating in community initiatives, partnering with neighbor organizations, and providing venues for involving the college community in current events and issues"—it is primarily through the curriculum and through service-learning "that students, faculty and staff will become responsible citizens, active community participants, agents of change, and visionary thinkers in an evolving and diverse society." As one President noted, "...one way... we teach good citizenship... is through our service-learning program." The dominant approach among the campuses in this study is through "combining classroom instruction with service activity"—or service-learning.

Service-learning appears compelling because it fulfills strategic goals: As one application noted: "In meeting goals, classroom learning activities engage students in campus/community partnerships, teach the application of theoretically based knowledge in the contemporary work world, and promote development of a lifelong commitment to civic responsibility." Also, campuses are gathering data that reinforces the strategic choice of service-learning. As one example, a campus reported data from a "post-service survey" where "83.1% of the students responding to the survey felt that they had an improved sense of civic and social responsibility as a result of their service-learning experience" and that the survey data indicated that "service-learning participation increased students' knowledge of civic and community needs and where to go for solutions." A number of campuses used the Community College Survey of Student Engagement (CCSSE) data as a way to assess the effectiveness of service-learning courses. As one campus reported: "93% feel that they can make a difference in their community" and "87% feel that their service-learning experience helped make them more aware of community needs." Service-learning also was able to address "college-wide competencies – including 'social and civic responsibility.'"

In the 2012 report, *A Crucible Moment*, the claim is made that for higher education, the goal should be that "education for democracy and civic responsibility is pervasive, not partial; central, not peripheral" (p. 2). The applications indicate that the primary means of implementing civic engagement to fulfill the civic mission of engaged community colleges is through service-learning. At the same time, even for campuses that have been classified as community-engaged, the data provided on the percentage of courses, faculty, and students involved with service-learning indicates that is not occurring to a great extent. For all the campuses, the average number of courses designated as service-learning courses, as a percent of total courses offered, is 9.6%. The average number of faculty teaching service-learning courses as a percentage of all faculty is 17.5%, and the average number of students participating in a service-learning course as a percentage of all students is 15.7%. The data from the Carnegie applications is consistent with CCSSE data – which is fairly consistent from year to year – "More than three-quarters of CCSSE respondents say that they have not participated in a community-based project as part of a course" (Center for Community College Student Engagement, 2012, p. 22). As the central strategy for institutionalizing civic engagement in community colleges, it appears that service-learning is not pervasive or central.

Additionally, while service-learning as a pedagogical practice is prominent in the applications, evidence of student civic learning outcomes is weak. Few campuses demonstrated the link between community-engaged pedagogical practices and student learning outcomes. If community colleges are fulfilling their civic missions through the curriculum by means of implementation of service-learning, then it appears that more attention needs to be given to student learning outcomes and the assessment of those civic outcomes if community colleges are going to be able to authentically and convincingly claim a civic mission that translates to civic learning.

Also, because the context suggests that the mission is operationalized through the curriculum, community engagement in the curriculum should be examined more carefully. What the Carnegie data reveal is the extent of activity, not the quality of the activity. Additional study should examine the intentionality of the civic dimensions that are included in pedagogy and curricular design. Additionally, the degree to which the faculty, often majority contingent, align themselves with the mission is critical to operationalizing the mission; it is important to analyze hiring, faculty professional development, and faculty rewards in greater depth to understand the connections between faculty culture and institutional identity.

Workforce Development and Civic Engagement

Evidence from the classification applications suggests that civic engagement and workforce development are not oppositional goals, but that the kind of learning and skills development that occurs through community-based experiences reinforces workforce and career preparation. In fact, application responses linked civic engagement to student advancement in "workforce and careers," referenced experiences in the community leading to "students getting jobs," and service-learning experiences leading to "more career insights." This kind of awareness of the linkages between community engagement and workforce preparation echoes the findings of Battistoni and Longo in their 2005 study, Connecting Workforce Development and Civic Engagement, which found that "colleges and universities can connect work and citizenship. Colleges and universities can be places where students learn to become both strong citizens and productive workers. Put simply, workforce development and civic engagement can be complementary visions for the future of higher education" (p. 5). The evidence from the applications also reinforces the civic expressions through occupations and careers explored by Boyte in his conceptualization of "public work," where citizens are not clients or consumers of politics and the state, but are public problem solvers and co-producers of public goods in all facets of their lives, including their occupations and professions (Boyte, 1996, 2013).

What is apparent in the classifications studied here is that "democracy colleges" take seriously the social justice imperative of preparing for a career and earning a living wage as an important aspect of allowing for active participating in democracy. One dimension of this could be thought of as the "economic capital" framing of a Community College education. Numerous studies show that access to higher education degree completion leads to a significant lifetime wage differential compared to those who graduate from high school only. Succeeding in higher education is the opening to opportunity and social mobility and contributing to a vibrant economy. The push for degree completion as an economic development imperative gets expressed as the need for workers who can compete globally and make the American economy the envy of the world.

In addition to economic capital, there is the "human capital" dimension of a community college education. Productive and innovative workers have a well-rounded set of competencies and social and personal attributes, are well educated in the arts and humanities, contribute to the production of culture, and these qualities are embodied in a such a way as to contribute to the ability to perform work that produces economic value. Democracy colleges are contributing to economic capital through human capital.

Table 1.3: Characteristics of Democracy Colleges

Institutional Identity	Outcomes	Capital Development
Democratizing Role (mandate)	Social Mobility Access Opportunity	Economic Capital
Civic function (mission)	Preparation for life, work, and civic participation	Human Capital
Public engagement that operationalizes the mandate and mission (practice)	A. Understanding civic institutions B. Practical experience with activity in the public arena (service-learning)	Civic Capital

Additionally, a key contribution of a "democracy college," in concert with contributing to the development of economic capital through the development of human capital, is the development of "civic capital." Civic capital is developed through education for civic agency. There is an emerging literature that describes civic agency as involving:

> . . . the capacities of citizens to work collaboratively across differences like partisan ideology, faith traditions, income, geography and ethnicity to address common challenges, solve problems, and create common ground. Civic agency requires a set of individual skills, knowledge, and predispositions. Civic agency also involves questions of institutional design, particularly how to constitute groups and institutions for sustainable collective action. Civic agency can be seen from a cultural vantage as the practices, habits, norms, symbols, and ways of life that enhance or

diminish capacities for collective action. This emerging body of knowledge and set of collective practices provide models for a major higher education initiative that will transform previous sources of civic decline into wellsprings of civic renewal and regeneration (Boyte, 2007).

The development of civic agency is particularly significant for community colleges because the students are predominantly local/regional. They come from the local community and they will go back to the local community. As a civic institution, the community college is preparing future civic leaders and active citizens. Civically engaged community colleges are developing the student civic agency and contributing to civic capital.

With these added dimensions of economic, human, and civic capital, it is possible to consider revision of the earlier framing of democracy colleges as a way of understanding what makes these colleges distinctive.

Civic Capital

Finally, the analysis of community colleges as "democracy colleges" suggests, perhaps, new insights into what it means to be an "anchor institution." Many anchor institutions have strong civic engagement commitments and demonstrate their effectiveness through economic impact. Often this is framed in terms of economic development, employment, and procurement – in terms of economic capital. How much this kind of civic engagement contributes to civic capital is unclear. Higher education institutions such as community colleges—and public regional comprehensive four-year campuses – are focused more on human and civic capital as well as economic capital in preparing students as future civic participants in local communities, what the American Association of State Colleges and Universities calls an institutional commitment to being a "steward of place" (2003).

Emergent Issues

A number of issues have emerged from analysis of the Carnegie applications that cannot be addressed through the data provided in the applications but should be considered. It may be worth analyzing whether the campuses represented in the Carnegie data are emblematic of an "elite" status within the community college sector that is shaped by political context and funding structures in state systems leading to level of sophistication in community engagement that is distinctive from other community college campuses. What are the factors that lead to this degree of resource allocation and sophistication?

It is important to understand the contextual factors and/or internal conditions that support civic engagement at community colleges. To what extent do contextual factors (institutional history; public support for higher education within the state, region, and local communities; workforce conditions; and level of complexity of state system of higher education) support the ways in which civic engagement is enacted within a given campus? Specifically, factors such as the collective bargaining context, percentages of contingent faculty, faculty teaching loads, the extensiveness of systemic support (e.g., state-level policy, resource allocation as controlled by the state), the extent of public support for public higher education in states with more extensive, well-articulated higher education systems, all could be examined to better understand the larger internal and external environments creating democracy colleges.

Recommendations

Based on the findings and analysis from this study, what do the Carnegie Classification applications submitted by community colleges reveal about the conditions under which civic engagement is enacted? How can community colleges deepen their efforts to develop the civic agency of their students and strengthen their roles in the democratic life of their communities?

We offer the following recommendations along with guiding questions to frame institutional decision making and planning. Examples of campus practice for each recommendation are provided from evidence in the applications.

Recommendation #1: Intentionally allocate institutional resources targeted at developing institutional capacity for civic engagement.

Campus can approach this strategy by addressing questions about the extent to which institutional resources are consistently allocated to support the development of civic engagement work. How are such structural models operationalized? What does it mean to intentionally allocate institutional resources targeted at developing institutional capacity for civic engagement? Practices from the applications include:

- Office space for service-learning unit
- Salary for service-learning staff

- Funds for travel to conferences and/or other meetings related to civic work
- Community-wide surveys of assets/needs related to community development
- Campus buildings located in community settings.

Recommendation #2: Catalyze Curricular Innovation.

Here the guiding questions to drive strategy are: To what extent is the institution already committed to its curriculum (including workforce development, liberal arts/transfer, short-term training, distance learning) as the central source of innovation? How does the college link its "local" identity to social justice issues in the curriculum as part of the evolving of the mission of the institution?

Practices from the applications include the following:

- Interdisciplinary first-year curriculum
- Learning communities
- Experiential learning communities focused on developmental curricula
- Extensive efforts to support cultural diversity, e.g., deliberative dialogues; climate surveys
- Participation in national efforts to achieve equity (e.g., Achieving the Dream - ATD)
- Consistent commitment of vision and resources from senior leadership over an extended period of time

Recommendation #3: Build an Institutional Culture of Engagement.

Here, the campus can approach this strategy with the questions: Is civic engagement deep and pervasive, reaching across all levels of the campus? Are there policies, structures and practices that support civic engagement efforts? Is a priority for civic engagement integrated with other institutional priorities (student success, completion, workforce preparation, student-centered learning)?

Building community engagement into the institutional culture requires multiple interventions simultaneously. The examples provided here are from multiple applications. The ability to change culture would be reliant on enacting a number of these practices on a single campus at the same time:

Examples from the applications include:

- Multiple forms of formal and informal assessment of community needs which are integrated into college, department, and program-level planning.
- Program review:
- Accreditation
  - Campus Compact membership;
  - Campus Compact Indicators of Engagement status
  - Formal membership in The Democracy Commitment
  - Opportunities for careful deliberation over assessment outcomes from national instruments (e.g., CCSSE, BSSE, AtD data)
- Linking student learning outcomes related to civic work with other efforts to document student learning campus-wide.
- Faculty development to build faculty capacity for pedagogical practices and student learning outcomes that address civic engagement.
- Explicit articulation of civic engagement in hiring of faculty and in promotion of faculty (tenure track and non-tenure track).
- Efforts to document service-learning engagement on academic transcripts of student work.

Recommendation #4: Build an Institutional Identity and Commitment to Civic Engagement.

The recommendation is related to the one above to build a culture of civic engagement, but it raises different questions to guide strategy: To what extent are readily accessible symbols of commitment to civic engagement available for appreciation by the public? What organizational artifacts suggest a sustained commitment to civic engagement?

There is a wide range of examples of practices from the applications:

- Standing committees devoted to civic work.
- Consistent and visible demonstration of leadership in the service of forging close, reciprocally reinforcing relationships between campuses and communities, particularly on the part of the President and senior staff as well as faculty leaders.
- Highly visible offices committed to service-learning with dedicated staff resources.
- Readily accessible public statements re-commitment to civic work.
- System of symbols of engaged work.
- Regalia for faculty and students at graduation signifying a commitment to service-learning.
- Notations in college catalog of service-learning designated courses.

- Presidential awards for civic engagement (for students, faculty, staff, community partners).
- National or regional designations acknowledging civic work (e.g. Campus Compact Impact Awards).

Recommendation #5: Re-claim the Civic Potential of Service-learning.

The evidence from the Classification applications indicates that service-learning is perhaps the most significant strategy for implementing the civic mission of engaged Community Colleges. It has the benefit of making a link between the curriculum and the desired student outcome of social and civic responsibility. As a curricular strategy, it is also an effective way of structuring civic engagement to align with the student population and student characteristics at community colleges.

It is also apparent from the evidence provided in the applications that service-learning is not pervasive in the curriculum as an opportunity widely available to students across the college. There is also little evidence of service-learning being tied to civic learning outcomes, or ways to articulate and assess the civic learning of students. The absence of the identification and assessment of civic learning outcomes suggests that service-learning needs to be enhanced with robust civic engagement practices if it is to reach its civic potential. Service-learning, as a pedagogical method lacking civic intentionality, will not prepare students for civic engagement or lead to civic learning outcomes (Saltmarsh, 2005).

This is not a matter of moving beyond service-learning. The problem is not with service-learning per se. The fundamental pedagogical approach is sound: through learner-centered approaches that validate the knowledge and experiences of students and partners in communities, students participate in experiences in a community and reflect on those experiences and the course content in order to better understand social issues and how to act as problem solvers with others in addressing public issues. Yet service-learning, to achieve its civic potential, must be more than a pedagogical method, and more than a curricular approach of implementing the pedagogy in courses across the disciplines. Simply as a pedagogical tool, service-learning becomes a way of teaching the course content more effectively. What is needed is to embed the civic in the course content.

Perhaps it would be productive to think of service-learning as being a foundation for civic engagement, but what is needed in addition to, or to be built upon, is civic scaffolding above the foundation to be able to achieve civic learning and engagement.

One possible level of scaffolding is through dialogue and deliberation as an approach for bringing civic engagement into the curriculum. While there has been extensive development of dialogue and deliberation (sometimes referred to simply as deliberation, or as deliberative dialogue) as effective approaches for public problem-solving in communities, only more recently has there been attention to the implications for higher education as a site for dialogue and deliberation as a way of educating for effective participation in a democracy (Thomas, 2010).

According to the National Coalition for Dialogue and Deliberation, a dialogue process "allows people, usually in small groups, to share their perspectives and experiences with one another about difficult issues [in ways that] dispels stereotypes, builds trust and enables people to be open to perspectives that are very different from their own." Deliberation "emphasizes the importance of examining options and trade-offs to make better decisions . . . about important public issues [through a] process that involves all parties and explores all options" (National Center for Dialogue and Deliberation).

Dialogue and deliberation build democratic skills and deeper understanding of public issues and can lead to individual and collective action on public issues – or what we think about as civic engagement. According to Longo, when deliberation is connected to teaching and learning as a "deliberative pedagogy," this often takes place inside the boundaries of a classroom. An example of this is where "a faculty member might use public deliberation to help students understand the nature of public policy choices, to develop skills in group communication, or to understand a specific public issue" (2013, p. 51).

Deeper civic learning and engagement can occur when dialogue and deliberation are scaffolded onto service-learning. Longo argues for "public deliberation" to be "joined by more widely publicly engaged practices – such as service-learning . . . that help to educate for civic responsibility outside the walls of the campus" (p. 49-50). When service-learning is combined with deliberation, then service-learning can more effectively lead to student civic learning and engagement. When Longo calls for "deliberative dialogue that connects with education in the community," (p. 50) he is making a case for building the scaffolding of deliberation on the foundation of service-learning to educate for civic engagement.

Another possible level of scaffolding is through "critical civic literacy," a curricular approach that has been implemented at California State University at Monterey Bay, where service-learning is a required part of the core curriculum. From the perspective of a critique of service-learning as reductionism to pedagogical method, critical civic literacy is scaffolding of civic learning and engagement that builds upon a foundation of service-learning. Critical civic literacy, writes Pollack, "recognizes that our new globalized, technologized, and highly unequal world requires community members to possess a new set of civic skills so that they are sensitive to diversity, aware of the role of power relations, and skilled in intercultural communication" (2013, p. 232).

According to Pollack, critical civic literacy "examine questions related to power, inequality, justice, and social responsibility in the context of [a] specific field of study"(p. 226) and "emphasizes the role that social power plays in facilitating or inhibiting meaningful participation by individuals and/or groups in public processes " (p. 231). What would this look like in comparison to a typical service-learning course?

For example, in the traditional paradigm, a service-learning course in computer science or information technology might focus on students bringing a variety of new computer-related solutions to community organizations, applying the knowledge they have learned in their majors to address real community needs around technology. The students might be doing service using technology; but are they learning about service and social responsibility or inequality or justice? From a critical civic literacy perspective, curriculum development begins with the identification of a key social justice issue related to technology, such as the "digital divide." The digital divide then becomes the organizing theme for the course, and student learning focuses on questions such as "How has digital technology accentuated or alleviated historic inequalities in our community?" And "what is my responsibility for addressing the "digital divide" as a future IT professional (p. 234)?"

With the scaffolding of critical civic literacy, "students examine issues of power, privilege, oppression, a systematic inequity in service-learning courses" (p. 231). In this way, service-learning can be used for civic learning and engagement.

The metaphor of scaffolding—scaffolding civic learning and engagement on a foundation of service-learning—also allows for consideration of ways to integrate approaches. Much like the findings from Kuh's studies of "high impact practices" that engage student in learning—e.g., first-year experiences, study abroad, learning communities, service-learning, capstones—where he found that greater impact came from combining approaches – e.g. a first-year experience course designed as a learning community using service-learning (Kuh, 2008), perhaps the same case could be made for scaffolding civic learning and engagement approaches on a foundation of service-learning. What would be the civic learning and engagement outcomes from a course that connected service-learning to deliberation and to critical civic literacy? Service-learning allows for connections to and relationships with community members outside the academy. This is essential but not sufficient for civic learning and engagement. For service-learning to achieve its civic promise, it needs to be combined with approaches that teach the knowledge and skills of democratic engagement.

Conclusion

Community colleges committed to civic engagement align their complex public purposes with a core mission of educating students as effective civic actors contributing to improving the communities that the campus and students are a part of. As part of their public mandate, historic mission, and curricular practice, community colleges are developing student economic, human, and civic capital. As a primary strategy for operationalizing a civic mission, campuses have embraced service-learning as a pedagogical and curricular approach. While this is a potentially effective strategy, and one that accounts for the student, faculty, institutional, and community context, there needs to be more attention to using service-learning as a foundation or platform for civic learning and engagement. A scaffolding of civic skills and knowledge can be built on the foundation of service-learning in such a way that more attention can be given to civic learning outcomes and ways to assess outcomes to determine what civic learning and engagement is occurring through a community college education. Civically-engaged community colleges offer promise in demonstrating new models of democracy colleges to be examined, adapted, and emulated across higher education.

References:

American Association of State Colleges and Universities. (2003). *Stepping forward as stewards of place: A guide for leading public engagement at state colleges and universities*. Washington, DC; American Association of State Colleges and Universities.

Battistoni, R.M.& Longo, N. (2005). *Connecting Workforce Development and Civic Engagement: Higher Education as Public Good and Private Gain.* North Shore Community College Public Policy Institute.

Boyte, H. C. (1996). *Building America: The democratic promise of public work.* Philadelphia, PA: Temple University Press.

Boyte, H. C. (2007). Building civic agency: The public-work approach. *Open Democracy.* November. Retrieved from https://www.opendemocracy.net/en/building_civic_agency_the_public_work_approach.

Boyte, H. C. (2013). *Reinventing citizenship as public work: Citizen-centered democracy and the empowerment gap.* Dayton, Ohio: The Kettering Foundation.

Center for Community College Student Engagement. (2010) *The heart of student success: Teaching, learning, and college completion (2010 CCSSE Findings).* Austin, TX: The University of Texas at Austin, Community College Leadership Program.

Center for Community College Student Engagement. (2012) *A matter of degrees: Promising practices for community colleges student success (A first look).* Austin, TX: The University of Texas at Austin, Community College Leadership Program.

Kuh, G. D. (2008). *High-impact educational practices: What they are, who has access to them, and why they matter.* Washington, DC: Association of American Colleges and Universities.

Longo, N. V. (2013). Deliberative pedagogy and the community: Making the connection. *Higher Education Exchange,* pp. 49-59.

McClenney, K. M. (2007). Research update: The Community College Survey of Student Engagement." *Community College Review.* 35; p. 137.

National Center for Dialogue and Deliberation. http://ncdd.org/rc/what-are-dd

The National Task Force on Civic Learning and Democratic Engagement. (2012). *A crucible moment: College learning and democracy's future.* Association of American Colleges and Universities.

Pollack, S. (2013). Critical civic literacy: Knowledge at the intersection of career and community. *Journal of General Education.* 62.4. p. 223-237.

Saltmarsh, J. (2005). The civic promise of service-learning," *Liberal Education,* Spring, Vol. 91, No. 2, p. 50-55.

Sturm, S., Eatman, T., Saltmarsh, J., & Bush, A. (2011). *Full participation: Building the architecture for diversity and public engagement in higher education* (White paper). Columbia University Law School: Center for Institutional and Social Change.

Thomas, N. L., ed. (2010). *Educating for deliberative democracy*. New Directions in Higher Education series. Berkeley, CA: Jossey-Bass.

Zlotkowski, E., Duffy, D. K., Franco, R., Gelmon, S. B., Norvell, K. H., Meeropol, J., & Jones, S.G. (2004). *The Community's College: Indicators of Engagement at Two-Year Institutions.* Providence, RI: Campus Compact.

Chapter 2

BLENDING CIVIC AND CAREER EDUCATION IN THE "IN-BETWEEN" SPACES

The Minneapolis College Example

Lena Jones
Minneapolis College
Minneapolis, Minnesota

This chapter tells the story of the Community Development A.S. degree program at Minneapolis College. It describes the city that birthed the program, the program's roots in Minneapolis' Native American community, and its curriculum. It also describes the advantages and disadvantages of the program's position in the "in-between" spaces at the college—between disciplines, between liberal arts and career programs, and between academia and community. Though the details may be uncommon, the story of this program offers broadly applicable lessons about the possibilities of integrating civic and career education at community and technical colleges and suggests ways that institutions can prepare for the challenges of creating and sustaining such programs.

Context: Our School and Our City

Minneapolis Community and Technical College (MCTC) is an urban campus on the northeastern boundary of downtown Minneapolis, Minnesota. The College is the result of a 1996 merger between Minneapolis Technical College, founded in 1914, and Minneapolis Community College, an open enrollment liberal arts institution established in 1965. The College offers 114 Associates degrees, certificates, and diplomas housed in the College's eight schools: Business and Economics; Design and the Arts; Education; Information Technology; Liberal Arts and Cultures; Nursing, Health Sciences and Public Services; Science and Mathematics; and Trade Technologies.[1]

The college is a commuter campus with 6704 students enrolled during Spring semester 2019, with the majority of our students residing in the Minneapolis neighborhoods that surround the college.[2] Our student body is racially diverse with 55% students of color or indigenous. The average age of our students is 27. 66 % of our students attend part-time, 74% major in Liberal Arts fields, and 49% are eligible for Pell grants.

Table 2.1: Demographic Data- Minneapolis Community and Technical College (Spring 2019)

Race/Ethnicity	Percent
American Indian/Alaska Native	1%
Asian	5%
Black or African American	30%
Hispanic or Latino	13%
Native Hawaiian/Other Pacific Islander	.1%
Non-Resident Alien	2%
Two or More Races	7%
Unknown	3%
White	38%

Our city, Minneapolis, has a population of slightly over 380,000 and is part of the seven-county Twin Cities Metropolitan area, which has a population of over three million (Metropolitan Council, 2017). This metropolitan area includes the state capitol, St. Paul, MN, which has a population of over 300,000.

While the Twin Cities and Minnesota rank well overall on a variety of indicators such as unemployment and poverty rates, educational attainment, homeownership, the Twin Cities and the state has some of the largest disparities in the US between its white population and its communities of color in all of those indicators (DEED Labor Market Information Office, n.d.; McCann 2020; Minnesota Budget Bits, 2010; Minnesota Compass, n.d.).

The Community Development Program: Its Origins and Its Worldview

The Community Development A.S. degree program at MCTC aims to prepare students for a wide range of careers in non-profit organizations, community development corporations, government, and the private sector, all of which are connected to the aim of bringing about community change. It also aims to create leaders that make "a difference in people's lives, working to improve urban communities and affecting change through policymaking at local, state and federal levels" by providing students with the practical skills to research community development issues, an understanding of approaches, methods, and techniques used by community developers...," and skills in leadership and teamwork.[3]

The Program, which became operational in 2010, originated in the Phillips neighborhood of Minneapolis, the birthplace of the American Indian Movement and home of a significant portion of Minneapolis' Native American population. Leaders from the Native American Community Development Institute (NACDI), an alliance of Native American nonprofits and businesses located in the Phillips neighborhood, recognized the need for a "new generation" of Native American leaders with community organizing and community development skills and created the program in collaboration with faculty members and administrators at MCTC. The program strongly reflects the vision of Sydney Beane, co-founder of the NACDI as well as a long-time community organizer and community developer, filmmaker, and instructor of several of the program's core classes until 2016. The indigenous focus of the program is largely due to Beane, who was born on the Flandreau Santee Sioux Reservation in South Dakota and is from a family who was exiled from Minnesota after the 1862 Dakota war.

The program's indigenous, community development emphasis manifests in several ways. The first is reflected in its support for the development of leaders who are rooted in the communities that they aim to transform. This is a primary reason why MCTC, an institution with students who primarily come from neighborhoods in Minneapolis, was chosen by the program's founders as the base for the program.

On a deeper level, the indigenous emphasis is reflected in the program's holistic world view, which emphasizes the interconnectedness of things and the need to create spaces for seeing and understanding power and analyzing the systems of control that divide people and communities from one another. In the words of Beane, these systems of control lead people to "accept the containment of problems" and the existence of "great wealth and poverty" in their communities and the world, amongst other things. To bring about the change that enables people to collectively protect and maintain the things that sustain us, Beane adds, one must understand how to organize people and resources within the context of conflicting worldviews and develop the courage to imagine and work towards "another reality that doesn't have to accept those separations" (S. Beane, 2016).

One way that the Community Development program challenges "separation" thinking is through encouraging students to reflect upon their higher education journey beyond individual goals and accomplishments. This is done by creating curricular and extra-curricular spaces for students to build meaningful relationships with one another, faculty, and community partners, to *collectively* think about their vision for their campus, city, state, and country, and to craft a career and life journey that feeds into that vision. At a practical level, this visioning process also involves helping students identify their talents and passions, explore vocations that would help them make a living *and* work towards their collective and individual goals, identify specific skills that they need to develop, and devise strategies for developing those skills inside and outside of the program. Many of the activities used to pursue these aims in the core courses and outside of the classroom (through the Community Development Student Organization, for example) draw heavily from various community organizing and popular education traditions.

The program's original core courses, developed in 2008 by Beane and Justin Huenemann (also of NACDI), largely focused on community development project management. However, in 2010, Beane and I redesigned the curriculum to better reflect the mission of the program.[4] The core courses in the redesigned curriculum include (new courses in bold):

- *Community Development and Indigenous Cultures*

- ***Community Organizing- History, Theory and Practice***
- ***Politics, Media and Community Organizing: Indigenous Understandings and Practices***
- *State and Local Government*
- ***Introduction to Public Policy***
- ***Leadership and the Politics of Community Change*** and
- ***Political Science Field Study***

The remainder of the program's required courses are in the business department and a variety of liberal arts disciplines. The program also has 18 elective credits that give students the ability to choose a variety of courses tailored to their specific interests, educational goals (Ex: transfer) and career goals.

The Challenges of Living in the "In-Between"

As noted in the introduction, the Community Development program has tended to occupy the "in-between" spaces at my institution. While this has offered opportunities for creativity and freedom, it has also brought about challenges that highlight the difficulties of surviving in such spaces in higher education.

The Structural Challenges of Interdisciplinarity at the Program Level:

New academic programs, especially those that do not fit neatly into well-established disciplines, need to be frequently fed and watered in order to survive. The journey of this program illustrates the difficulty of providing this nourishment within institutional structures built to support and perpetuate disciplinary boundaries.

Funding structures at MCTC only allow for budgetary support to go to academic programs that align with well-established disciplines. By "well-established," I am referring to disciplines that are common across higher education institutions and that usually have courses with designators that reflect the discipline (Ex: The Human Services A.S. program has Human Services (HSER) courses; the Psychology A.A. program has Psychology (PSYC) courses, etc.). The Community Development A.S. program is comprised of a set of core classes housed in American Indian Studies and Political Science along with additional required classes in a variety of departments. The practical consequences for interdisciplinary programs such as this one is that they only survive if there is a dedicated faculty member who is willing to take on coordination duties (promoting the program, recruiting students, supporting students once they are in the program, maintain partnerships with community partners, making sure the core classes are offered, making sure academic advisors knew about and had accurate information about the program) without compensation for that work from the college. Since there are no "Community Development" courses, there is no institutional funding for the program beyond the instructional costs of running its core classes.

The Challenge of Disciplinary Structures and Academic Credentialing at the Course Level

From the beginning, program leaders grappled with the conflicting realities that the knowledge needed to engage in transformative social change work transcends disciplines and that for a course to exist within an academic institution, it must live in a discipline. When Beane and I redesigned the program, we concluded that political science would be a good home for most of the core courses due to the fact that I was a tenured faculty member who was willing to use my institutional power to make sure that courses were offered on a regular basis and maintain meaningful connections with community partners and issues so that the program and its courses remained relevant.

One of the key aims of the program is to create a constantly evolving body of knowledge that reflects the best insights from inside and outside of academia. One of the primary ways it seeks to do this is through hiring adjunct instructors currently working in the field to teach some of its core courses. However, increasingly rigid credentialing requirements within the Minnesota State system have made it more difficult for those without a degree in the specific discipline where a course is housed to teach courses. This problem arose with Leadership and the Politics of Community Change, a political science course that was created in collaboration with Twin Cities Public Allies.

After having taught the course for a couple of years, Antonio Cardona, the regular instructor, who was the Director of Public Allies and co-creator of the course, was deemed ineligible to teach the course by the Minnesota State system office because his Master's Degree was in Public Administration and not Political Science. This was dispite his many years of direct experience related to the content of the course. It wasn't until the Political Science Department was assigned a new dean who was willing to push for an exception to this ruling that Mr. Cardona was able to resume teaching the class after a one-year hiatus. Interestingly, the current credentialing requirements would prevent Beane and Huenemann, the program's founders who both have graduate degrees in disciplines other than American Indian Studies or Political Science, from teaching the core courses of the program.

The Career and Technical Education (CTE)/ Liberal Arts Divide

Many community and technical colleges are the result of the melding of Liberal Arts Associate's degree granting institutions and institutions that grant career and technical degrees and certificates geared towards a particular profession. In the 2016 article, "Bridging the Workforce and Civic Missions of Community Colleges," I note the potential for collaboration and learning between liberal arts and CTE faculty at blended institutions, particularly in the area of experiential learning (Jones, 2016). However, divides between liberal arts and career and technical programs are still deeply embedded in the norms and structures of many community and technical colleges such as mine, making attempts to transcend these divides challenging.

For example, in 2013, MCTC launched an initiative called *MCTC Works!* that sought to bring together faculty across the college to develop a college-wide approach to internships in community-based learning. This initiative faced challenges in the implementation phase due to funding rules attached to the grant that supported the initiative. Specifically, the two staff members assigned to the project were restricted from officially working with non-CTE programs such as Community Development because their positions were funded by a federal Perkins grant. The elimination of a full-time service-learning coordinator position 2012 made the lack of support for experiential learning in non-CTE programs even more dire.

The Community Development program's struggle for recognition within the institution also illustrates the challenges inherent in bridging the liberal arts/CTE divide. In the program's redesign, Beane and I intentionally decided to locate the program's core courses in liberal arts departments (Ex: Political Science, American Indian Studies) while building in features typically found in career and technical programs (such as an advisory committee and a field study/internship requirement). We chose this route to offer students a highly transferable degree that also explicitly and intentionally prepared students for a vocational journey. However, due to its hybrid nature, the program was neither classified as a Liberal Arts or CTE program.

The consequence was that the program, though operational, didn't "exist" in several key areas of the institution. Specifically, because the program wasn't classified within the existing Liberal Arts/CTE structure, it was simply left off of institutional research reports, institutional assessment projects, and academic advising materials in its early days. The program eventually came to "exist" within these institutional structures due to the persistent efforts of core course faculty members, students, and community partners and the eventual decision to classify the program as a career program.[5]

The Advantages of Living in the "In-Between" spaces

The structural position of the program within the institution, and the limited resources it receives as a result, makes it necessary for us to think and act as organizers in the sense of constantly and intentionally widening and deepening our web of relationships within and outside of the institution and analyzing the internal and external power dynamics that affect the quality and sustainability of the program. In a sense, we are forced to practice what we teach in order to survive.

Building and cultivating partnerships:

Due to the program's roots in the broader community, and the challenges it has faced gaining institutional support due to its interdisciplinary nature, partnerships with organizations outside of academia have been central to this program from its outset. Beyond NACDI, the program has relied upon an advisory committee comprised of individuals from various types of non-profit organizations, government, and bachelor-degree granting institutions to help shape the curriculum, identify potential field placement and employment opportunities for students, raise money for the program and its students, and advocate for the program within and outside of the college.

In its early years, the program was able to survive without support from the college's general fund due to its relationships with non-profit organizations, which have supplied the program with monetary and human resources. For example, Community Learning Partnership, a national network of Community Change Studies programs with a mission of developing a "workforce of community change agents"[16] supported 3-8 credits of teaching release time for a faculty member to coordinate the program for several semesters between Fall 2011 and Spring 2017. In addition, the Native American Community Development Institute

(NACDI) and Pillsbury United Communities, in partnership with CLP and program faculty, have had some success raising funds to provide stipends to Community Development students while they are fulfilling their field study requirement.

Student as Partners

The creativity necessary to survive in the "in-between" has also shaped a culture that sees students as partners in the process of shaping their educational experiences and the program itself. This culture is rooted in our recognition of students as people with whom we are connected beyond the classroom as fellow residents of our neighborhoods, city and state and not just as people who happen to be taking our classes. Our program's students, who are 74% part-time, 65% over 25, and close to 70% students of color/indigenous and low income (MCTC Office of Strategy, Planning and Accountability, 2018), bring an incredible amount of wisdom, relationships, experience and drive that we would be foolish not to tap.

From the program's beginning, the Community Development Student Club (renamed the Community Development Student Organization in 2016) has been a key partner in building and sustaining the program. The organization was created in 2012 by students in the program's first cohort who saw the need for a space beyond the classroom for them to build relationships with one another and practice the skills that they learned in the classroom. Throughout its history, the student organization has frequently held forums on topics related to the program curriculum and has strategically scheduled most of these events during the times that the core classes in the program are held. In the absence of institutional funding for the Community Development program itself to hold such events, the student organization has greatly increased out-of-the-classroom educational opportunities for students in the program.

Students are also encouraged to participate in the Community Development Program Advisory Committee meetings. During these meetings, which bring together the program's community and higher education partners two or three times per year, students get to participate in conversations about the state of the program, program curriculum, the activities of our partners, and opportunities for collaboration. These meetings also provide students with the opportunity to directly connect with our community partners.

Table 2.2 An Example Degree Program at Minneapolis College

Minneapolis College School of Nursing, Health Sciences, and Public Service Community Development A.S. Program	
Curriculum (60 Credits)	**Partners**
Core Courses *Political Science Courses:* • Community Organizing: History, Theory, and Practice • Politics, Media, and Community Organizing • State and Local Government • Introduction to Public Policy • Leadership and the Politics of Community Change* • Political Science Field Study *American Indian Studies Courses:* • Community Development and Indigenous Cultures *Business Courses:* • Small Business Management* **Other Required Courses** • College English • Information Literacy and Research Skills • Intro to Global Studies • Intro to Sociology • General Psychology • Ethnic America • Intercultural Communications **18 Elective Credits** *Students choose electives geared towards their educational and career goals*	**External Partners** • *Community Learning Partnership (CLP)*- a national network of community change studies programs • *Advisory Committee Members* Government (Ex: Hennepin County; City of Minneapolis; City of St. Paul) Higher Education (Ex: Metropolitan State University) Non-profit organizations (Ex: Native American Community Development Institute-NACDI) • *Field Study Sites* (Ex: Hennepin County, Harrison Neighborhood Association, American Indian Community Development Corporation, St. Paul Parks and Recreation, Afro-Eco, Minneapolis Downtown Improvement District) **Internal Partners** • *Community Development Student Organization (CDSO)* • *Career Services Office* • *Other Programs within the School of Nursing, Health Sciences, and Public Service*
*the degree requires students to take either of these courses	

Conclusion: Successes and Challenges

As of Spring 2019, the Community Development program has 20 graduates and many others have become part of our community due to having taken our core courses and/or participating in the student organization. Students have gone on to work in government and non-profit organizations and create their own businesses and organizations. For example, Abdirahman Muse, one of the founding members of the Community Development Student Club and 2015 graduate of the Community Development Program, served as a Senior Policy Aide for Minneapolis Mayor Betsy Hodges, became the Executive Director of the Awood Center for East African Workers, and was appointed by Minnesota Governor Tim Walz to the Metropolitan Council, a regional planning authority for the 7-county Twin Cities metropolitan area.

Say Yang, a 2018 graduate of the program, acquired a position with the Hennepin County Department of Housing, Community Works and Transit while still a student in the program and currently serves as the Program Coordinator of the Center for Earth, Energy and Democracy, a leading organization in national environmental justice work. Lisa Owen, 2015 graduate, co-founded *Adobe DeSigns*, a business in South Minneapolis that won the National Association of Minority Contractors Small Contractor of the Year Award in 2015 and the Neighborhood Development Center's New Business of the Year Award in 2016. The business has created signs for sites such as US Bank Stadium, Hennepin County, and Minneapolis-St. Paul International Airport. Though I end this chapter highlighting some of our successes, it is important to note the challenges that remain for us as we approach the 8th year after the program's redesign. While we no longer need to worry about the program being excluded from institutional research reports or academic advisors disseminating inaccurate information, the grant funding that had historically supported the coordination of the program through buying course release time has dried up. Given the multi-year declines in enrollment and revenue at the college, the prospects of receiving hard institutional funds for this coordination work in the immediate future are practically zero. This is making it more challenging for me and other faculty associated with the program to provide the same kind of intensive support and one-on-one mentorship that we have provided for our students in the past, given the heavy course loads of full-time community college faculty. The continued success and viability of the program and its students depends on our ability to mobilize our relationships with internal (Ex: Career Services) and external (Ex: Advisory Committee, Alumni) partners to support our students in their journeys.

What are the key lessons that can be drawn from our experience? To successfully create and grow such programs, essential ingredients are internal and external advocates with institutional power and access to resources, including funding. Such advocates in our case were key administrators, tenured faculty, and local and national community partners willing to work collaboratively and use their knowledge of institutional processes and relationships to make the program a reality.

Now that the program is established, the challenge has shifted to sustaining the program without the "start-up" funding that the program had in its early days. That support included grants acquired by community partners that were used to develop curriculum, build partnerships, pay guest speakers, fund field experiences and professional development activities for students in the program, and purchase faculty time to coordinate and promote the program. Those needs continue, however, as dollars from our college's general fund have not replaced the grant funds that once supported these essential activities. At the moment, the program is largely surviving on the passion, interest, and creativity of key deans, staff, faculty, community partners, alumni, and current students who have a stake in the program's existence and are willing to work together. While we recognize that the current situation is not ideal, we are hopeful that our continued work in the "in-between" will transform our college in ways that will strengthen holistic and transformational civic and career education at our institution and beyond.

Notes

1. Please see https://www.minneapolis.edu/academics
2. This is based on my analysis of student zip code data, acquired from the MCTC Office of Strategic Priorities and Accountability in December 2018.
3. Please see https://www.minneapolis.edu/community-development.
4. Syd Beane and I co-designed the courses in bold in 2010. The Community Development and Indigenous Cultures course was part of the original set of core courses and State and Local Government was an existing course that was added to the core curriculum.
5. The source of the decision to classify the program as a career program and the exact timing of this classification remains a mystery. Sydney Beane and I only discovered this when an administrator encouraged us

to apply for Perkins funding in 2016. The full consequences of this classification remains to be seen. Though we are now included in institutional reports, the change has yet to result in any funding from Perkins or any other sources.
6. For more information, please see http://www.communitylearningpartnership.org/

References

Beane, S. (May, 2016). Indigenous framework of the community development program." (L. Jones, interviewer). Retrieved from https://www.youtube.com/watch?v=OYZbIOaPudM&feature=youtu.be.

DEED Labor Market Information Office. (n.d.). Twin Cities metro regional disparities by race and origin. Retrieved from https://mn.gov/deed/assets/041018_tc_disparities_tcm1045-341196.pdf.

Jones, L. (2016). Bridging the workforce and civic missions of community colleges. *New directions for community colleges*, 173, 121-129.

McCann, A. (January 14, 2020). States with the most racial progress. *WalletHub*. Retrieved from https://wallethub.com/edu/states-with-the-most-and-least-racial-progress/18428/.

MCTC Office of Strategy, Planning and Accountability. (2018, August 22). Count of student by major: MnSCU operational data report.

Metropolitan Council. (2017, March 23). Population growth in the 7-county metro remains strong; Carver County surpasses 100,000. Retrieved from https://metrocouncil.org/News-Events/Communities/News-Articles/Population-growth-in-the-7-county-metro-remains-st.aspx.

Minnesota Budget Bites. (2018, September 13). More new census data shows Minnesota's prosperity isn't reaching all Minnesotans. Retrieved from http://www.minnesotabudgetbites.org/2018/09/13/more-new-census-data-shows-minnesotas-prosperity-isnt-reaching-all-minnesotans/.

Minnesota Compass. Disparities: Overview. (n.d.). Retrieved from https://www.mncompass.org/disparities/overview.

Chapter 3

CIVIC AND COMMUNITY ENGAGEMENT AFTER THE SUMMER OF HATE

Connie Jorgensen
Piedmont Virginia Community College
Charlottesville, VA

This chapter focuses on the ways in which civic engagement, especially the encouragement of civil dialogue, has become an institutional priority at Piedmont Virginia Community College (PVCC). Specifically, we explore the effect that the events of August 12 & 13, 2017, the "Summer of Hate," had on the college community. We also consider legislative mandates and how civic engagement fits into the college mission. Finally, we detail some strategies that the college is instituting to increase its emphasis on incorporating civic issues into the curriculum.

PVCC is a small community college located in Charlottesville, Virginia. It serves students from Albemarle, Buckingham, Fluvanna, Greene, Louisa and Nelson Counties and the city of Charlottesville. In 2018-2019, PVCC served 2,797 full-time equivalent students (FTEs) (an unduplicated headcount of 7,178 students). The student population taking classes for credit at PVCC is 58% female, 32% minority, 26% under the age of 18 and 29% age 25 and older, and 88% part-time (*PVCC Office of Institutional Research, Planning, and Institutional Effectiveness*, 2019).

Legislative Mandates

Virginia law mandates that higher education graduates be prepared for civic engagement. The "Goals of the Virginia Plan for Higher Education" (2014) Goal #2, requires that the State Council of Higher Education for Virginia (SCHEV) provide a framework for student success by "[ensuring] that graduates are prepared with the competencies necessary for employment and civic engagement." The 2017 SCHEV *Policy on Student Learning Assessment and Quality in Undergraduate Education* grew out of this goal and further mandates that institutions define each of the four SCHEV general education competencies, of which civic engagement is one, and determine assessment measures.

Civic engagement was identified by SCHEV and the Virgnia Community College System (VCCS) as one of the six new general education competencies. PVCC's *Strategic Plan 2018* lists civic engagement under "Goal 1: Increase Student Success and Completion" with the strategy to "Implement the revised VCCS General Education Outcomes in all degree programs" and the critical task of "incorporate[ing] in all degree programs and assess[ing] student learning outcomes in **civic engagement**..." (p.6) *[emphasis added]*. In this sense, civic engagement is an integral part of the institutional planning process.

PVCC Mission and Values

PVCC's mission and values align with and provide support for the topic of civic engagement. As the community's college, PVCC views civic engagement as an essential aspect of the College's mission and vision. PVCC's mission is to offer "accessible, affordable, high-quality educational programs that promote student success and **community vitality** [emphasis added]." Community vitality refers to the growth and prosperity of the communities where our graduates will live and work. PVCC's community impact value statement is that "we develop innovative programs to meet the changing needs of our students and the business community while contributing to the economic, **civic**, and cultural vitality of **our region, the Commonwealth of Virginia, our nation, and the world**" [emphasis added] ("Mission & Goals," n.d.). Supporting and engaging with the community is foundational to PVCC; therefore, it is the College's goal that graduates see this as important too.

The decision to focus college resources on civic engagement was also driven by data received from institutional planning and assessment. The results from The Democracy Commitment's 2017 Civic Engagement

Survey showed that 69% (n=99) of students had not taken a political science or government course at college. The *Community College Impact on Student's Civic Engagement* report stated that 47% (n=68) of students had not taken a course that deals with social, political, or economic inequality. In addition, results from The Democracy Commitment's 2018 Civic Engagement Survey shows that only 65.57% of students occasionally or hardly ever were actively involved in political or social issues.

Because of these data, SCHEV and VCCS policies, and the Unite the Right rally, PVCC has increased its commitment to civic engagement and civil dialogue to encourage our students to discuss difficult issues in a well-reasoned and civil manner. We want our students to be able to critically assess evidence and factual claims and construct clear arguments, as well as being active in the local community. These efforts, we believe, will reduce the chances of conflict among the students we serve, and help them become leaders in the community.

The Summer of Hate

The event that sparked PVCC's increased emphasis on civic engagement was what Charlottesville journalist Hawes Spencer describes as *The Summer of Hate* (Spencer, 2018). During the summer of 2017, Charlottesville's Lee Park and its statue of Confederate General Robert E. Lee were the site of numerous rallies by various groups of white supremacists and counter-protesters as the community debated whether or not to remove the statue. In August, Heather Heyer and two Virginia State Troopers were killed at the Unite the Right Rally.

PVCC's Response: New Civic Learning Program Initiatives

Following the Unite the Right Rally, the community was stunned, saddened, and galvanized to action. Frank Friedman, president of Piedmont Virginia Community College, made the following commitment on behalf of the College: "It is now a time for healing and for our community to come together. PVCC will be an active partner in promoting tolerance and diversity in our community in the days ahead." (Friedman, 2017).

Panels, Teach-ins, and Conferences

Even before the August 2017 Unite the Right Rally and accompanying violence, PVCC had been reconsidering and adjusting its civic engagement efforts to provide an opportunity for our students to learn and discuss tough issues like the proposal to remove Confederate monuments. In response to these heightening tensions, PVCC included a panel titled "What to do with Charlottesville's Confederate Monuments" in our 2017 Civic Leadership Conference. We sought panelists who would represent the spectrum of opinion on the issue – leaving them in place, adding "context" to them in place, or removing them. The students responded favorably to this discussion; in fact, this was the best-reviewed event of the conference.

When the PVCC community returned to classes for the Fall 2017 semester after the alarming events of the summer, faculty, staff, and students were still traumatized by the violence and hatred that had disrupted our community. Faculty met to strategize ways in which to discuss what happened in our classes and in co-curricular activities. In the second week of classes, faculty hosted a teach-in about the racism and anti-Semitism that had been exposed during the summer. The event was very well attended by students, faculty, and staff. Many of the attendees expressed a desire for additional forums, especially those including civil discussions about difficult issues.

Faculty developed writing assignments to address the events of the summer in their course work and participated in college-sponsored trainings designed to help them facilitate the difficult what were sure to arise in their classroom.

The annual Civic Engagement Conference, which engages PVCC students with the community around controversial ideas, intensified its focus on engaging with difficult subjects. Panels included Guns in Schools, Charlottesville's Racial Divide, MeToo: United Online, Where Do We Go From Here? and The Uses and Abuses of History. We also integrated Deliberative Dialogue into the schedule (see description below).

The Human Library

Another response to Summer 2017 was The Human Library™, which is designed to build a positive framework for conversation that challenges stereotypes and prejudices through dialogue. In the Human Library, students become "books" which other students check out in order to hear their stories. PVCC conducts a Human Library™ event annually during Banned Books Week. This project involves students, faculty, and the community. Previous "books" raved about the experience: "I highly recommend that PVCC students become a human library book!" wrote student and Human Library 'book' Kathleen. "It is a great way to meet some of your fellow students and getting ready to be the 'book' lets you take a look at your reasons for being at PVCC, as well as your near and long-term goals. When students 'read' your story, you typically learn things about them as well. All in all, it is a great experience."

One Book

PVCC's One Book program at Piedmont Virginia Community College is an institution-wide initiative held to bring together students, faculty, staff, and members of the community to all read the same book and take part in activities inspired by the text. Through a variety of activities linked to the book and offered to the whole college, One Book strives to increase engagement and interdisciplinary dialogue among participants. The One Book program has committed to choosing books with civic engagement themes for the next several years. Our most recent book was *The Sixth Extinction* by Elizabeth Kolbert and in Fall 2019 it will be Michelle Alexander's *The New Jim Crow: Mass Incarceration in the Age of Colorblindness*.

Deliberative Dialogue

In 2017-2018, PVCC participated in a pilot project with the Kettering Foundation on promoting Deliberative Dialogue in community colleges. Since then PVCC has been developing a robust Deliberative Dialogue program that encourages participants to consider multiple perspectives and look for common ground for action. Dialogues are led by trained faculty, staff, and student moderators, and use an issue discussion guide that frames the issue by presenting an overview, followed by three or four broad approaches to solving the problem.

Last year, PVCC offered two campus-wide Deliberative Dialogues – one about immigration the other about climate change. Moving forward, the college aims to make Deliberative Dialogue a hallmark of the PVCC student experience, offering at least two college-wide Deliberative Dialogues per academic year, linked to current issues and events like One Book [fall semester] and the Civic Engagement Conference [spring semester]. Additionally, by training teaching faculty and students each year to be Deliberative Dialogue facilitators, we hope to increase the number of students experiencing Deliberative Dialogue in the classroom.

Incorporating Civic Engagement into the Fabric of PVCC

PVCC hosts numerous events on campus focused on civic engagement, including Constitution Day, Free Speech Week, Banned Books Week, and National Voter Registration Day. Since August 12, 2017, the focus shifted to topics that emphasize freedom of speech, the value of diverse viewpoints, respect for diversity, and social equality.

For example, our 2017 and 2018 Constitution Day topics were "Race and the Constitution" and "The Cost of Free Speech." For Free Speech Week in 2018, we asked the question "Should free speech survive August 12?" And in 2017 we responded to the wave of campuses disinviting controversial speakers with a discussion about "Free Speech on Campus".

Several committees and campus organizations have created their own discussion forums as well. For example, the Diversity and Inclusion Committee holds monthly Diversity Dialogues open to all faculty and staff. The Student Government Association will be coordinating a college-wide service project that includes speakers and discussions about the source of the problem they are addressing and possible solutions.

In addition, our Student Development courses will offer a civic engagement and voting module and the English faculty will require a writing assignment based on a public issue and an information module.

The QEP and PVCC's new Civic Engagement Vision

PVCC's new Quality Enhancement Plan (QEP) *Civic Sense: Engaging students in the Civic Life of our Communities* was approved in October 2019 and is bringing all this work together under one plan. During the planning process in 2018/19, the Summer of 2017 was in everyone's mind. The planning team decided the goal of the plan should be stated in the following way: "Because of their experiences at PVCC, graduates will be more likely to be civically engaged." A broader Civic Engagement Vision Statement was developed that articulated:

> PVCC's civic engagement efforts seek to build student leaders who have a strong commitment to democracy and diversity, and who engage in the civic life of their communities through collaborative, creative, and critical problem-solving.

To meet the QEP goal, the team developed the following student learning outcomes:

- SLO 1. Graduates will actively participate in civic life by voting in local, state, and federal elections.
- SLO 2. Graduates will actively participate in civic life by engaging in public service or other activities that improve the condition of communities and/or the quality of people's lives.
- SLO 3. Graduates will evaluate multiple perspectives to think critically about issues of public consequence.

Civic Engagement Course Designation

A new component of PVCC's civic engagement culture is the incorporation of the Civic Engagement (CE) course designation. These courses will be offered in each degree area and will be the culminating curricular civic engagement experience, allowing students a sustained engagement with a public problem or issue. Each CE course will include a substantive project (up to 25% of the course grade). This will not require an additional credit toward graduation. The CE part of the class will be integrated into the existing class structure.

As the college moves forward with the QEP, significant resources will be available to support the plans. An assessment plan is in the works to survey students about their level of civic engagement both in student development courses and when they leave (via the graduation survey).

Professional Development

In order to make all this happen, PVCC has committed to increased opportunities for professional development, especially for faculty. Faculty will be expected to model civic engagement, make connections between their disciplines and issues of public consequence, and consider how to build civic engagement into their courses.

The College reserves one week prior to the beginning of each semester for information sharing, planning, and professional development. Civic engagement will be a focus of college planning weeks for at least the next five years. For the first three years, the College will bring in a keynote speaker who will address faculty and staff on a civic engagement topic. The College will also offer workshops during convocation weeks on topics such as incorporating Deliberative Dialogue into courses, designing civic engagement activities, and using strategies for introducing students to civic engagement.

- Voting Quiz in the required Student Development Course
- National Study of Learning, Voting, and Engagement

- Virginia Voting Survey
- Student Satisfaction Survey
- Civic Engagement Rubric
- Feedback Surveys

Conclusion

In conclusion, several factors led PVCC to increase its civic engagement efforts, including the Summer of Hate, legislative mandates, and the college mission. These factors led to the development of our Quality Enhancement Plan. Over the next five years, PVCC is committed to improving our civic engagement presence on campus and integrating CE into the fabric of the college. We have significant buy-in from faculty, staff, administration, and students as well as additional resources to support the effort. Because of the high level of support from across the college community, we are optimistic about our plans. Our biggest challenge is to make the QEP work. We look forward to doing great things!

References

Bauman, D. (2018). After 2016 election, campus hate crimes semed to jump. Here's what the data tell us." *Chronicle of Higher Education, February 16, 2018.* Retrieved from https://www.chronicle.com/article/After-2016-Election-Campus/242577

Friedman, F. (2017). Official PVCC statement in response to "Unite the Right" rally in Charlottesville. Retrieved from https://www.pvcc.edu/news/2017/08/14/official-pvcc-statement-response-unite-right-rally-charlottesville

PVCC Office of Institutional Research, Planning, and Institutional Effectiveness (2019, June 11). PVCC annual student enrollment summary. Retrieved from https://www.pvcc.edu/sites/default/files/2019-08/Annual%20Enrollment%20Summary%2018_19.pdf

Spencer, H. (2018). *Summer of Hate: Charlottesville USA.* Charlottesville, University of Virginia Press.

Chapter 4

CIVIC ASSESSMENT AT DELTA COLLEGE

Measuring Change in Political Interest, Civic Attitudes, and Likelihood of Future Participation

Lisa Lawrason
Delta College
Saginaw, MI

Delta College is one of America's leading community colleges in civic learning. It is one of the original 23 signatory institutions to *The Democracy Commitment* (now Community Colleges for Democracy), an association of community colleges dedicated to preparing students for active citizenship. It has earned distinction as a Voter-Friendly Campus by Campus Vote Project and partners with other national organizations to politically empower students. Various initiatives across campus, both inside and outside the classroom, create civic encounters for students to become aware of how politics impacts their lives and their role in shaping the world in which they live.

Delta College requires students pursuing an A.A. or A.S. degree to earn one credit of civic engagement or take a service-learning-designated course. This entails 15 hours of volunteering in the civic life of the student's community. (The service-learning option is embedded in the course and does not require 15 hours outside of class.) While any faculty member can attach a one-credit civic engagement component to their course, most students earn this credit through POL105, American

Politics with Project. The course outcomes and objectives for POL105 are identical to that of POL103, American Politics, with the addition of the 15 hours of civic engagement in POL105. Importantly, Delta College also requires a 3-credit foundational civic literacy course, which can be fulfilled with several different of political science or history courses.

Given the additional effort – both on the part of students and faculty – to engage students in public activity, political science faculty sought to measure the impact of the civic engagement project on civic attitudes, political interest and likelihood of future participation. The college offers both an Americans politics survey course with the project (POL105) and without the project (POL103), creating a natural experimental setting to test the impact of 15 hours of civic engagement. Both POL105 and POL103 students completed pre and posttests measuring their civic attitudes at the beginning and end of the course. A civic index was created as a composite of items on the pre and posttests, with the difference calculated and compared in both groups.

The results discussed in this chapter demonstrate a statistically significant difference in POL105 and POL103 students, with those completing the civic engagement project demonstrating more positive civic attitudes, greater growth in political interest and a stronger likelihood of future political participation. For community colleges seeking to grow their students' sense of civic agency, this chapter provides evidence that a hands-on civic engagement project has potential to move students toward becoming active citizens.

Background of Civic Engagement Graduation Requirement

The civic engagement graduation requirement came out of a committee that was charged by the Vice President of Instruction and Learning Services to revise and strengthen degree requirements while aligning with the Michigan Transfer Agreement, which at the time was in its infancy. This committee was comprised of faculty representatives from each of the eight academic divisions across campus. At the time, the graduation requirements for the AA and AS degrees had not been changed for 15 years. Also noteworthy was the college's progress toward establishing service-learning as a teaching pedagogy across disciplines. The college's membership in Campus Compact, along with dynamic faculty passionate about service-learning, created a fertile environment that led to faculty across disciplines incorporating this teaching pedagogy into their classes. Because the infrastructure for service-learning and civic engagement was already in place at the college, requiring either service-learning or civic engagement seemed a logical and doable next step.

Within this context, the Lumina Foundation released its Degree Qualifications Profile, prompting colleges to reconsider the definition of what graduates should be able to do and know at the associate's level. The Lumina Foundation's Degree Qualifications Profile lists civic and global learning as one of five categories of learning outcomes or proficiencies (Adelman et al., 2014) These degree profiles reflect learning outcomes that all students – regardless of major field of study – should master in order to thrive in today's dynamic and complex work environment. The Civic and Global Learning category acknowledges the foundational purpose of higher education to train students as citizens. At the associate's level in this category, the report recommends students provide "evidence of participation in a community project through either a spoken or written narrative that identifies the civic issues encountered and personal insights gained from this experience" (Adelson et al., 2014, p. 19).

In light of these recommendations, the newly emerging Michigan Transfer Agreement and the existing infrastructure for service-learning and civic engagement, the graduation requirements committee proposed, among other changes, that students meet both the civic literacy *and* civic engagement requirements for AA and AS degrees. The recommendation passed with 88 percent of faculty in agreement.

Theoretical Foundations

The goal of the civic engagement graduation requirement at Delta College is to prepare students for democratic citizenship, while at the same time to develop soft skills that employers are looking for. Specifically, it requires students not only to learn about their role in a democratic society, but also to actively participate for 15 hours in civic life. Faculty individually design the project for their courses, creating variation among the projects. Examples of civic work in which students might engage include working on election campaigns, designing and implementing an issue awareness campaign, participating in voter registration drives, and visiting the state capitol to talk with lawmakers about issues of concern. These projects force students to step outside their private lives and into the public realm, a prospect that is intimidating for many. Key to these experiences is that students are not volunteering in isolation of the social, political or economic context of the problem that they are addressing but are working to identify root causes of problems and develop policy solutions.

Given the additional effort—both on the part of students and faculty—to engage students in public activity, political science faculty began seeking a method to measure the benefits of civic engagement, compared to mere civic literacy. Are students gaining a greater understanding of their community and a greater likelihood of engaging in the political realm through the civic engagement project? Are they gaining a mental predisposition that is favorable toward participating in the civic lives of their communities? If transforming students into active citizens could be accomplished without the civic engagement project, through in-classroom only experiences, such as they receive in POL103, then there would be little justification for the civic engagement project or graduation requirement. Through a pre and posttest measuring political interest, civic attitudes and future participation, the political science discipline assessment compared the change in attitudes from the start to the end of the semester, in POL103 and POL105 students.

The survey instrument is designed to capture students' political interests and attitudes toward political participation. With political interest being the greatest predictor of political knowledge and participation (Delli Carpini & Keeter, 1996; Verba, Schlozman,& Brady, 1995), identifying interventions that set students on a path toward political interest could be of great value to democracy. Political interest is an attitude toward an object, that object not being the political world itself, but one's involvement in the political world. This distinction is essential for conceptualizing how civic engagement can reduce psychological barriers to students' viewing themselves as someone who engages politically. Civic engagement projects within the classroom context have great potential to challenge students' preconceived ideas about politics. They can shatter students' stereotypes about politics and their perception that it's "not for people like me." The pre and posttests are designed to measure change in students' mental predispositions toward engaging in the political world, even if that attitude has not yet manifested into action outside of the course context. If a person is curious about politics, that psychological predisposition may manifest into spectator-like actions such as talking about politics and seeking political news, or more demanding actions such as voting, donating money or campaigning on behalf of a candidate. It is entirely possible, however, that political interest will not immediately manifest into more taxing activities. Those who are politically interested, however, should look favorably upon engaging in those more demanding activities.

Understanding the source of political interest is of great concern to those attempting to solve the puzzle of why some engage while others remain spectators in the American political system. This intrinsic curiosity about politics (van Deth, 1990) begins to crystalize for people in their 20s (Prior 2009), around the time when students attending colleges and universities may be required to take an American politics course. These courses are required with the objectives of getting students to become more knowledgeable about public affairs, more interested in and more active in politics, and more effective as citizens. College instructors, thus, have the job of molding citizens through a one-semester political science course required for graduation. Yet most students who end up in introductory American politics survey courses at Delta College have bypassed traditional paths for fostering political interest, such as politically interested parents (Verba, Schlozman & Brady, 1995), engaged social networks (Kolter-Berkowitz, 2005) and civically-cultured K-12 school settings (Hess and Torney, 1968). Indeed, a survey conducted of 229 Delta College students in 2014 found that when asked if they follow "what's going on in government and public affairs most of the time, whether there's an election going on or not," 56 percent said "hardly at all" or "only now and then." Only 11 percent of the sample answered "most of the time" (Lawrason, 2015). The sample of students for this study overwhelmingly characterized politics as boring, intimidating, and complex and certainly not worth their time to figure out. This is an important insight for those who educate community college students to assume the role democracy demands of them. These students must be convinced that their attention to and participation in politics matters.

Acquiring political interest is a prerequisite to democratically-favorable attitudes, skills, and behaviors and is essential if students are to engage in the political process throughout life. Such engagement helps ensure that there is a government that represents their interests and values. Thus, understanding the paths by which students become politically interested and ultimately participate in politics lends insights into the quality and equality of representative government in the United States.

The focus on measuring political interest and likelihood of future participation is a unique approach to student assessment, grounded in the online processing model, which posits that attitudes persist much longer than facts. Long after the learned facts fade from memory, the attitude shaped by those facts remains (Baum, 2003; McGraw et al., 1990). In the same way, political science researchers agree that a knowledgeable electorate is theoretically good for democracy but lack a consensus on what set of facts are essential for good citizenship: Institutions and processes? Issues and policies? History? Current political alignments? (Delli Carpini & Keeter, 1993). Indeed, cultivating an interest in politics and favorable civic attitudes has potential to motivate students to seek out political information and become more politically-knowledgeable citizens (Luskin, 1990).

With this theoretical foundation, the Delta College political science discipline developed an instrument to measure political interest, civic attitudes, and likelihood of future political participation. Some of the measures were adapted from The Civic and Political Health of the Nation Report (Keeter et al., 2002), while others are common measures found in the American National Election Study. This assessment was administered to 11 classes—five POL103 and six POL105—in the fall 2017 and fall 2018 semesters. The dataset includes 98 students who completed the American politics course with the civic engagement project (POL105) and 105 students who completed the American politics course without the project (POL103). This sample of students—all of which saw the same civic literacy objectives, while only some completed the project—provides a natural experimental setting to test the effects of the civic engagement project on civic attitudes. Analysis of the results demonstrates a statistically significant difference in the difference between pretest and posttest results measuring political interest, civic attitudes and likelihood of future political participation when comparing students in both courses, with POL105 students demonstrating more positive civic attitudes and behaviors.

Assessment Design

The civic assessment is comprised of 15 questions on a five-point Likert scale, ranging from strongly agree (1) to strongly disagree (5), as well as four 4 questions on a 10-point scale. Two separate indexes were created by adding students' scores on each of these sets of questions for the pretest and posttest. The Likert scale questions are designed to measure student's current orientations toward participating in the civic lives of their communities, as well as the likelihood of future participation. These questions include the following:

1. I have a good understanding of the needs and problems facing the community in which I live.
2. Politics is relevant to my life.
3. As a citizen of the United States, I can influence the affairs of governments around the world.
4. In the future, I am likely to work together with someone or some group to solve a problem in the community where I live.
5. In the future, I am likely to volunteer for community service (for no pay).
6. In the future, I see myself keeping track of issues facing my community on a regular basis.
7. In the next election, I am likely to display a button, sign, or stickers to promote a candidate, party, or issue.
8. In the future, I am likely to contact a local official—at any level of government—to express my opinion.
9. In the future, I am likely to boycott products manufactured by a certain company because I disagree with the social or political values of the company that produces it.
10. In the future, I will likely belong to or donate money to a group or association, either locally or nationally, such as a charity, labor union, professional association, political or social group, sports or youth group, and so forth.
11. We know that most people don't vote in all elections. To what extent do you agree with this statement: I will probably vote in the next election.
12. In the future, I am likely to start a petition to mobilize other people around an issue.
13. In the future, I am likely to contact a newspaper or news magazine to express my opinion on an issue.
14. In the future, I am likely to take part in a protest, march or demonstration.
15. In the future, I am likely to work as a canvasser – going door to door – for a political or social group or candidate.

A civic index was created by adding the total score for each survey respondent. As seen in the results below, a lower score on the civic index indicates more positive civic attitudes, with the responses coded as follows: strongly agree = 1; agree = 2; neither agree nor disagree = 3; disagree = 4; and strongly disagree = 5.

The questions in the civic index (above) represent the most common way social science research measures attitudes is through survey questions that ask respondents to self-report their attitudes toward a particular object. While this method is direct, the validity of these responses assumes that individuals can access their attitudes and are willing to honestly report them. This may or may not be true. Respondents may report the socially acceptable response so as to look good for the survey (for example, see Silver et al., 1986). An indirect method of measuring attitudes is to ask individuals to rank their preferences, with the assumption that attitudes influence these preferences. With this method, there is less propensity for respondents to worry about and try to give socially acceptable responses to a direct question about their attitudes. As such, the survey instrument asks four questions in which respondents indicate where they fall on a 10-point scale. These questions ask respondents to identify their personal interest in politics, how much they enjoy discussing politics, how much they enjoy learning about politics, and the extent to which they see themselves being politically involved in the future. The general question about political interest and the more specific question of political learning both tap into curiosity, while the question about political discussions and getting involved politically tap into engagement. The sum of responses from these four questions is then used to calculate a 40-point Political Interest Index.

> On a scale of 0 to 10 (0 being no interest and 10 being high interest), how interested would you say you personally are in politics? *Please circle the number.*
>
> 0   1   2   3   4   5   6   7   8   9   10
>
> On a scale of 0 to 10 (0 being no enjoyment and 10 being high enjoyment), how much would you say you enjoy *learning about politics*? *Please circle the number.*
>
> 0   1   2   3   4   5   6   7   8   9   10
>
> On a scale of 0 to 10 (0 being no enjoyment and 10 being high enjoyment), how much would you say you enjoy *discussing politics*? *Please circle the number.*
>
> 0   1   2   3   4   5   6   7   8   9   10
>
> On a scale of 0 to 10 (0 being strong disagreement and 10 being high agreement), indicate your level of agreement with the following statement: *I see myself as someone who could be involved politically. Please circle the number.*
>
> 0   1   2   3   4   5   6   7   8   9   10

Assessment Results: Comparing Changes in Civic Index Scores Between POL103 and POL105 Students

Because we are interested in measuring the *change* in civic attitudes, controlling for pretest scores is essential for detecting a significant difference between the students who completed a civic engagement project and those who did not. This method allows for the comparison of treatment effects within a participant in the study, as opposed to among all participants. In this way, each subject acts as their own control. Thus, any students for which we could not match pre and posttest scores were eliminated from the analysis. This includes those who may have been absent on the day either test was administered, or those who failed to write their name legibly on the assessment. A total of 203 cases remained.

Analysis of covariance is an appropriate statistical test to compare pre and posttest scores among two groups. This allows for comparing the difference in means in the posttest results from the two groups – POL103 and POL105 – controlling for the pretest scores. The Analysis of Covariance model, using pretest scores as a covariate, can be displayed as follows:

$y_1 = b_0 + b_1 * \text{Treatment} + b_2 * y_0 + e$

In the basic descriptive statics of the entire sample, split between POL103 and POL105, both the mean and median for the Pre-Civic Index were higher than that for the Post-Civic Index. (Recall that a lower score means more "strongly agrees" and "agrees" and thus demonstrates more positive civic attitudes.) Statistical insignificant difference in the pretest scores for POL103 and POL105 indicate that at the beginning of the semester, students enrolled in both classes demonstrated a relatively equal propensity toward engaging in the political word. In both POL103 and POL105, the mean and median on the Post-Civic Index is lower than the Pre-Civic Index, demonstrating more favorable civic attitudes at the end of the semester than at the beginning. However, the change in mean from pre to post for POL103 is 3.97 points, whereas the change in mean for POL105 is 5.73 points.

In the analysis of covariance, the difference in posttest means for POL103 and POL105 is significant when controlling for pretest scores. The significance-value for the POL103/105 independent variable is .034, significant at the .05 level.

Table 4.1 Comparing POL103 and POL105

		Pre Civic Index	Post Civic Index	Difference from Pre to Posttest
POL103 (without civic engagement project)	Mean Median	45.10 45.00	41.04 41.00	3.97 4.0
POL 105 (with civic engagement project)	Mean Median	46.61 45.00	40.84 40.00	5.73 5

The difference in post-test means for POL103 and POL105, controlling for pre-civic index scores, is more than 2 points, with the relationship in the expected direction: POL105 students exhibit lower scores, demonstrating more favorable civic attitudes at the end of the semester. The causal relationship is strong, significant at the .05 level.

Assessment Results: 40-point Political Interest Scale

Using the same ANCOVA model to measure differences in change in the 40-point political interest index yields a similar demonstrable difference in students who completed civic engagement projects and those who did not. (Note that unlike the above tables, a *higher* score on the 40-point political interest index indicates *more favorable* civic attitudes.) Whereas students in both courses started out with similar (statistically insignificant) levels of political interest; the end of the semester shows greater growth among the POL105 student than the POL103 students.

Table 4.2 Mean and Median for Pre and Post Political Interest Index

		Pre Political Interest Index	Post Political Interest Index	Difference from Pre to Posttest
POL103 (without civic engagement project)	Mean Median	18.17 17.00	21.83 23.00	3.38 3.0
POL105 (with civic engagement project)	Mean Median	18.07 18.00	24.95 25.00	6.60 7.00

Comparing the difference post-test means for the 40-point political interest index, while controlling for pretest scores, demonstrates a strong, statistically significant relationship between participating in a civic engagement project and growth in political interest. The mean difference in posttest scores between the POL103 and POL105 students was 3.391, when controlling for pretest scores. This difference between the two classes was significant at the .01 level.

Conclusion

In both statistical analyses conducted, completing the civic engagement project demonstrated a strong, statistically significant effect on students' change in their mental predisposition toward engaging in the civic lives of their communities. Students who completed the 15-hour project were significantly more likely to see themselves as agents for positive change in their community than those who completed the civic literacy requirement, without the hands-on engagement. Whereas no statistically significant difference emerged in students taking each class at the beginning of the semester, the greater growth in the POL105 students is powerful evidence of the more democratically desirable outcomes resulting from the civic engagement project. Once again, these results have implications for those interested in preparing community college students to become engaged citizens. Graduation requirements of many colleges and universities include political science courses, with the hope that they will foster skills and values necessary for active citizenship. For political science professors with this goal, understanding interventions with potential to heighten political interest and cultivate favorable civic attitudes is worthwhile. Civic engagement is one such intervention.

Previous research has demonstrated that today's young adults are more politically disinterested and ignorant than any other age group in the United States today, and perhaps more so than any other generation in the history of survey research (Wattenberg, 2012). This apolitical attitude is concerning because interest in politics to be the strongest predictor of political knowledge and participation (Delli Carpini & Keeter, 1996; Verba, Schlozman & Brady, 1995). Lacking experiences in their childhood and adolescence to cultivate political interest, many community college students have entered their formative years destined to a lifetime of alienation from the political system. These findings are concerning to those who believe that democracy works best when its citizens are informed and involved in their political system.

Employing assessment techniques that measure students' changes in interest in the political world and a propensity to become engaged may be more useful than measuring changes in factual knowledge. As supported by the online processing model, students' attitudes about their involvement in the civic life of their communities will remain long after they discard factual knowledge they gained from the class. When employing this assessment technique, there is much to celebrate in the impact of civic engagement *experiences* when comparing this pedagogical approach to that which emphasizes mere civic literacy.

References

Adelman, C., Ewell, P., Gaston, P., & Schneider, C.G. (2014). The degree qualifications profile. Lumina Foundation. Retrieved from https://www.luminafoundation.org/resources/dqp.

Baum, M. A. (2003a). Soft news and political knowledge: Evidence of absence or absence of evidence? *Political Communication, 20*, 173–190.

Delli Carpini, M. X. & Keeter, S. (1993). Measuring political knowledge: Putting first things first. *American Journal of Political Science.* 37: 1179-1206.

Delli Carpini, M. X. & Keeter, S. (1996). *What Americans know about politics and why it matters.* New Haven, CT: Yale University Press.

Hess, R. D. & Torney, J. (1968). *The development of political attitudes in children.* Garden City, NY: Anchor Books.

Lawrason, L. (2015). *Laughing our way to a stronger democracy: Political comedy's potential to equalize political interest and political knowledge in community college students.* PhD Dissertation, Wayne State University.

Luskin, R. C. (1990). Explaining political sophistication. *Political Behavior. 12(4):331-361.*

Keeter, S., Zukin, C., Andolina, M., & Jenkins, K. (2002). The civic and political health of the nation report. CIRCLE, accessed from https://civicyouth.org/PopUps/2006_CPHS_Report_update.pdf.

Kotler-Berkowitz, L. (2005). Friends and politics: Linking siverse friendship networks to political participation. In A.S. Zuckerman *(Ed.), The social logic of politics: Personal networks as contexts for political behavior* (pp. 152-170). Philadelphia, Penn.: Temple University Press.

McGaw, K., Lodge, M. & Stroh, P. (1990). On-line processing in candidate evaluation: The effect of issue order, issue importance, and sophistication. *Political Behavior* 12: 41-58.

Silver, B. D., Anderson, B. A. & Abramson, P. R. (1986). Who overreports voting? *The American Political Science Review* 80: 613-624.

Van Deth, J. (1990). Interest in politics. In M.K. Jennings and J.W. Van Deth (Eds.), *Continuities in political action: A longitudinal study of political orientations in three western democracies* (pp. 275-312). New York: W. de Gruyter.

Verba, S., Schlozman, K. L., & Brady, H. E. (1995). *Voice and equality: Civic voluntarism in American politics.* Cambridge, MA: Harvard University Press.

Wattenberg, M. P. (2012). *Is voting for young people?* Boston: Pearson Education.

Chapter 5

FORGING GUIDED PATHWAYS FOR CIVIC AND POLITICAL ENGAGEMENT

Developing a Partnership to Provide Civic Opportunities for Students That Span Their Enrollment at Two- and Four-Year Institutions

Sarah J. Diel-Hunt
Heartland Community College
Normal, Illinois

Stephen K. Hunt
Illinois State University
Normal, Illinois

In the face of criticism that many in higher education lost sight of civic education as they focused more on job preparation for students, the last 20-plus years have yielded numerous initiatives designed to promote civic learning and democratic engagement. As noted poignantly in *A Crucible Moment*, "higher education has a distinctive role to play in the renewal of US democracy" (National Task Force, 2012, p. 2). A growing number of campuses across the United States are implementing community- and service-based learning objectives into curricula and co-curricula (Butin, 2010; Musil, 2015; Saltmarsh, 2005; Smith,

Nowacek, & Bernstein, 2010; Westheimer & Kahne, 2004; Woolard, 2017).

As part of an effort to address the lack of education for democracy in higher education, the American Association of State Colleges and Universities (AASCU), Carnegie Foundation for the Advancement of Teaching, and *The New York Times* partnered to form the American Democracy Project (ADP) in 2003. The goal was "to produce college and university graduates who are equipped with the knowledge, skills, attitudes and experiences they need to be informed, engaged members of their communities" (American Association of State Colleges and Universities, 2018, para. 2). In 2011, the project expanded to include community colleges through the original formation of The Democracy Commitment (TDC), which expanded over seven years to include 100 community college campuses serving over one million students in 22 states.

Forging a Partnership

In the heart of central Illinois sit two institutions of higher education committed to civic education: Heartland Community College (HCC) and Illinois State University (ISU). Heartland is a two-year, comprehensive community college serving a district population of over 230,000 through 14 transfer and applied degree and 31 certificate programs. It serves approximately 5,000 credit students, with over 70% of those enrolled in transfer programs. Just one mile south on Main Street is Heartland's largest transfer partner, ISU, a 4-year public university which enrolls over 20,000 students (18,000 undergraduates).

Both institutions declare civic engagement as a core value. One of Heartland's five essential competencies is ethics and social responsibility, which includes learning outcomes assessment for student engagement in civic challenges at the local, national or global levels. Illinois State, as an original member of AACSU's Political Engagement Project (PEP), is one of only 50 US colleges to be named a Civic Learning and Democratic Engagement Leadership Institution. ISU has formalized its PEP with the following institutional goals:

1. Expand and update a curricular plan with student learning outcomes that will demonstrate increased student awareness of, and engagement in, political systems and processes past the first year.
2. Create and strengthen partnerships leading to more coordination between curricular and co-curricular activities to enhance political

activism by students, faculty and staff.
3. Encourage political activism in undergraduate students that leads to an increase in political leadership and participation on and off campus.
4. Develop students' understanding of political and social engagement as a life-long responsibility of all citizens.
5. Create and strengthen partnerships with other educational institutions and community leading to activities that enhance political activism by students, faculty and staff.

Both institutions also dedicate significant time, resources, and infrastructure to develop and support civic engagement initiatives and efforts, which are highlighted on their institutional websites.[1]

Given that the two institutions share a number of students through their extensive transfer programs, which include co-enrollment and matriculation, as well as a common commitment to civic engagement, it only makes sense that they would collaborate to create a guided pathway for the civic education of their students. However, no model for such partnership existed, which meant they had to innovate in order to move the two entities, with their own cultures and bureaucracies, toward a unique collaborative partnership that would create civic opportunities for students spanning their enrollment at the two institutions.

Civic and Political Engagement Collaboration in the Co-Curriculum

The Heartland/ISU civic engagement partnership began in 2008, when a Heartland administrator attended a PEP pre-conference planning session at the annual ADP conference (now called the Civic Learning and Democratic Engagement conference) with an Illinois State administrator. The meeting sparked conversation about collaborations between four-year colleges and universities and their community college transfer partners. Over the course of the next several years, Heartland and ISU developed numerous co-curricular partnerships.

The two institutions shared an interest in developing students' knowledge of local social and economic issues as well as the political infrastructure and landscape as a means to build motivation and skills for civic engagement in the Bloomington-Normal and surrounding communities. The first step was to integrate co-curricular programming. In order to facilitate joint planning, HCC maintained a representative on ISU's planning team, which met regularly. Additionally, joint planning meetings were held to collaborate with external partners, like the

League of Women Voters.

In 2008, Heartland and ISU deployed joint programming that included a "Trust Me, I'm a Voter" student-led campaign to facilitate voter education and registration ahead of the 2008 elections; work with community leaders through a group called the Living Democracy Committee to develop deliberative democracy skills in the community; congressional and local election town hall meetings; and a shared speaker who visited both campuses to discuss his documentary titled *18 in 08*. The initial efforts proved successful as Illinois State's larger budget and student population allowed Heartland to expand its efforts, while at the same time, Heartland's focus on "keeping it local" infused energy into local elections and issues that had previously gone unnoticed by the large college student population in Bloomington-Normal.

Table 5.1 Sample HCC/ISU Co-Curricular Civic Engagement Activities

Event	Description
What is the 21st Century Mission for our Public Schools?	Deliberative democracy forum in conjunction with the Living Democracy Committee.
Town Hall Meeting	Town hall event featuring U.S. Senator Mark Kirk and Congressman Adam Kinzinger.
Keynote Speech by Congressman Adam Kinzinger	Congressman Kinzinger visited with students as part of ISU's Communication Week.
11th Congressional District Debate	The debate featured Debbie Halvorson (D) and Adam Kinzinger (R) and was hosted at ISU.
Panel Discussion on NYC Islamic Center	The panel was held at HCC and featured HCC and ISU faculty.
Election Night Watch Party	HCC and ISU commonly co-host election night watch parties for local, state, and national elections.
State of the Union (SOTU) Watch Party	Like the election night watch parties, HCC and ISU also partner on Presidential State of the Union watch parties and tweet ups. In fact, HCC and ISU partnered in 2016 to serve as the national hub for President Obama's last SOTU address.

The partnership remained largely co-curricular in nature and included coordinated days of recognition on the two campuses, such as Constitution Day activities and joint speakers and panels, including one on the controversial topic of building a mosque at Ground Zero on the tenth anniversary of 9-11. Collaboration around voter information and registration activity also continued, including a straw poll for the 2012 elections showing results disaggregated by campus. These co-curricular partnerships were important to building the partnership and resulted in efficiencies of collaboration. Representatives from each institution met two to three times each semester and coordinated work with other local partners such as the McLean County Clerk, the League of Women Voters, and local media outlets. See Table 5.1 for a more detailed overview of these initiatives.

From Co-Curricular to Curricular Efforts

As co-curricular collaboration deepened and included avenues for faculty involvement in programming, attention turned to developing curricular partnerships. Illinois State, as a member of the AASCU PEP, had been developing its infrastructure for embedding civic and political engagement in the curriculum. Two key approaches included professional development for faculty and utilization of the general education program for delivery, particularly in the required general education course in communication.

Illinois State developed a course redesign program for faculty to embed civic and political engagement learning outcomes into existing curriculum. They offered that program to Heartland faculty, but that did not garner strong participation, so Heartland developed its own program, which is now offered as an online professional development certificate. Both programs are built on a similar concept: provide faculty compensated time combined with instruction to redesign their courses to include civic and political engagement outcomes and assessment.

Both institutions also chose to embed civic and political engagement learning outcomes in the general education curriculum for maximum student exposure. The introductory communication course is required in Illinois' state general education program, so both institutions revised that course to develop students' civic agency and skills necessary for meaningful participation in our democracy. Beyond the fact that nearly 3,600 students take the introductory communication course each year, there are many reasons why the course represents a critical site for integrating the pedagogy of political engagement. Initially, Hunt, Meyer, Hooker, Simonds, and Lippert (2016) argue that communication scholars and educators are uniquely positioned to foster civic agency and engagement, as meaningful participation in democracy rests on the foundation of communication competence. Further, Hunt et al. (2016) note that "in order to engage in political persuasion, students must have the verbal and argumentation skills needed to clearly articulate a position" (p. 120).

In her seminal study examining the effects of higher education on students' civic engagement, Hillygus (2005) found that the best predictor of future civic and political engagement was training in communication. Hillygus (2005) goes so far as to conclude that her findings "suggest that an educational system geared towards developing verbal and civic skills can encourage future participation in American democracy" (p. 41). Put another way, learning the skills of communication can go a long way in preparing students for future political engagement. Finally, Denton (2017) summarizes the relationship between communication and political engagement when he argues that the essence of politics is persuasive communication which forces us to "interpret, evaluate, and to act. Communication is the vehicle for human action" (p. xv).

ISU's introductory course, Communication as Critical Inquiry, and Heartland's Introduction to Oral Communication course both contain the following learning outcome: "effectively communicate in democratic situations, demonstrating the ability to consider and evaluate multiple perspectives on social issues and the ability to manage conflict." Both courses feature civic and political motivation and skill development and serve as a prime ground to link co-curricular programming through required participation in campus events and activities promoting civic and political engagement.

Assessment efforts were bolstered to track the impact of new civic and political engagement pedagogy on key student learning outcomes. In their examination of this pedagogy at ISU, Hunt et al. (2016) found that students participating in political and civic engagement pedagogies reported significantly higher means on measures of political knowledge, political efficacy, skills of influence and action, and anticipated future political behavior compared to students in control sections of the course. Importantly, Hunt et al. (2016) found no difference between the groups on a measure of political ideology. In other words, exposure to this pedagogy did not influence students' political beliefs or ideology.

In a previous study, Hunt, Simonds, and Simonds (2009) found that students learning through the PEP pedagogy in the introductory communication reported significantly highly means on measures of motivation as well as affect for the content of the course, behaviors recommended in the course, and the course instructor compared to students in control sections of the course. Put simply, students in political and civic engagement sections of the course were more motivated to study and liked the content and instructor of the course more than students in non-civic and political engagement sections. Taken together, these two studies provide empirical support for the inclusion of enhanced civic and political engagement pedagogy. Students receiving this instruction report substantially larger gains on measures of political engagement and actually report liking the course and instructor more than students in control sections of the introductory communication course.

Forging the Curricular Pathway

In 2011, ISU launched a minor in Civic Engagement & Responsibility (CER). The minor prepares students to participate in social change as well as develop an awareness of personal social responsibility. As an interdisciplinary minor, it is open to all students and can be positively matched with any major as a way to broaden the student's learning experience and career perspectives. The minor includes 21 credit hours, including nine core required courses:

- Foundations of Citizenship: An Introduction to Civic Responsibility
- Professional Practice: The Service-Learning Experience in Civic Engagement
- Citizenship and Governance

The CER minor also includes a concentration for teacher education majors who have an interest in urban education and pursuing careers in high-need schools.

With general curricular collaboration taking hold, ISU's development of the minor created an opportunity for HCC administrators to consider how they might create a pathway for students into this minor; however, while rules and guidelines exist for creating degree articulations, no framework existed for what such a pathway into a minor sequence of courses might look like.

After conferring with State of Illinois curriculum approval authorities, Heartland determined a curriculum sequence could be developed that, while not recognized as an official degree by the State, could be recognized by Heartland and transfer partners through articulation agreements. With that, Heartland worked to develop the Civic Engagement Curriculum Sequence (CECS), which included 15 credit hours, including 4 core required courses:

- ENGL 101: Composition I
- COMM 101: Introduction to Oral Communication
- POS 101: Introduction to Politics and Government
- POS 250: Activism

Elective courses included Introduction to Service-Learning, which could be taken for variable credit hours and up to five times for different experiences, including Alternative Spring Break (ASB), discipline-specific service-learning course sections, or independent service-learning in an area of passion for the student. With the curriculum in place at both institutions, Heartland and Illinois State then worked together to craft an agreement articulating HCC's CECS into the ISU CER minor.

Engaging Key Stakeholders

From the very beginning of the ADP/PEP and TDC initiatives, both campuses worked strategically to engage key stakeholders. For example, both campuses created implementation teams that included faculty and staff champions of civic and political engagement. Implementation team members played critical roles in recruiting faculty and graduate students, leading professional development, and developing new initiatives. At ISU, PEP efforts were brought under the umbrella of the campus ADP, which reported to the Provost and Vice President of Student Affairs. This alignment provided visibility for PEP activities to higher administration and bolstered the case for funding through ISU's budget process. At Heartland, civic engagement efforts were led by the Associate Vice President for Academic Affairs, who worked with key constituents in student engagement, academic affairs, instructional development, and assessment to plan for efforts that spanned the curriculum and co-curriculum.

As we noted in previous sections of this case study, ISU and HCC also worked diligently to engage stakeholders in the community. For instance, the McLean County Clerk was consulted regarding voter registration and education efforts. In addition, partnerships with groups like the League of Women Voters and the Living Democracy Committee were key for organization of panel discussions on local issues as well as election debates and town hall meetings. In an effort to expand connections with the community, ISU launched the Community Engaged Campus (CEC) initiative. The objective of the CEC was to build and maintain partnerships between campus and community. The partnerships took many forms and provided service-learning opportunities, construction of a web-based portal allowing community organizations to identify areas of need, and workshops for more than 60 partner organizations.

ISU and HCC administrators also worked closely together to build relationships with national ADP and TDC administrators. Both campuses have maintained active involvement in the Civic Learning and Democratic Engagement (CLDE) conference and have participated in new spin-off initiatives like the national study of campus climates for political learning spearheaded by the Institute for Democracy in Higher Education (IDHE). As mentioned previously, ISU and HCC have attempted to model partnerships between community colleges and universities through co-curricular activities like the State of the Union (SOTU) watch parties and tweet-ups. In fact, ISU and HCC served as the national hub for President Obama's 2016 SOTU address. More than 1,000 students, faculty, staff, and community members packed ISU's ballroom for the event. In addition, the watch party—which included pre-taped interviews with campus leaders, ADP and TDC staff, and political leaders—streamed live to more than 500 universities and community colleges across the nation. The watch party also featured a panel discussion following the SOTU with ISU and HCC administrators discussing collaboration between the two campuses.

In terms of the time commitment and budgetary support for our work, ISU provided a course reassignment for one faculty member to coordinate ADP and PEP activities. In addition, ISU administration provided financial support for PEP from both academic and student affairs. Further, the CER minor received significant financial support from the State Farm Companies Foundation. Other activities were funded through small grants from the McCormick Foundation. In fact, a McCormick Foundation grant provided financial support for workshops in fall 2018 that brought ISU and HCC faculty together with all other ADP-affiliated universities in Illinois to discuss strategies for embedding civic and political engagement into the curriculum of teacher education programs. At Heartland, the administration provided summer grant funding for faculty to infuse service-learning and civic engagement projects and outcomes into their courses and is currently providing a faculty member with a supplemental assignment to create an online professional development course for faculty to redesign their courses. Faculty will be paid to complete the course.

Challenges

As might be expected with any large initiative of this type, there were several challenges in integrating civic and political engagement into the curriculum and co-curriculum. Initially, recruitment of faculty was a challenge as some instructors see educating for democracy as outside the realm of their discipline, or possibly compromising their ability to adequately assess disciplinary content. Heartland and ISU sought to overcome this first by embedding political and civic engagement outcomes into their general education outcomes, but also by finding faculty champions to clearly communicate what is at stake if we turn our backs on the task of addressing political disengagement. Referring campus stakeholders to compelling scholarship indicating that infusing civic and political engagement into the curriculum and co-curriculum has a significant, positive effect on student learning outcomes also built buy-in. As previously noted, research in this area demonstrates that instructors can employ civic and political engagement pedagogy without altering students' political ideology. In addition, success can be found in reaching out to faculty who have demonstrated an interest in civic and political engagement through the classes they teach (e.g., courses related to social movements, policy issues, contemporary community issues, and the like).

Another challenge in recruiting faculty is related to their perceptions of the relevance of this work for tenure and promotion. ISU is engaging in discussions of adding language regarding the scholarship of engagement to the institution's tenure and promotion document. Heartland also privileges active learning and student engagement in its promotion criteria around instructional design and civic engagement, and service-learning pedagogies are featured in the new faculty onboarding academy as a great means of achieving this objective. In addition, both ISU and HCC have developed professional development initiatives around the pedagogy of civic and political engagement, including small grants and stipends for participating faculty. Beyond the grants and stipends, participation in these kinds of activities contributes to faculty teaching and research and helps build a case for tenure and promotion.

Without question, time represents a significant challenge for this work. Faculty can become overwhelmed with requests to participate in campus initiatives. In fact, some faculty members have expressed concern that they simply do not have the time to teach their curriculum and civic and political engagement simultaneously. We attempt to overcome this barrier by demonstrating the many ways in which this pedagogy overlaps with traditional liberal arts curriculum. For example, faculty directing the introductory communication course at ISU discovered that civic and political engagement pedagogy compliments the delivery of communication content. Faculty realize that teaching students how to communicate, think critically, evaluate information, and become more civically and politically engaged are mutually reinforcing and consistent with the long-standing goal of liberal arts education to produce well-rounded and engaged graduates.

Getting students excited about civic and political engagement can also be challenging. We have found that students are more receptive to this pedagogy when they perceive that the curricular and co-curricular activities are relevant to the content they are learning and their career goals. The assessment data collected in ISU's introductory communication course shed light on the impact of civic and political engagement pedagogy on students' motivation and attitudes toward the course and instructor. As noted earlier, Hunt et al. (2009) found that students who receive PEP pedagogy reported significantly higher means on measures of affective learning (i.e., attitudes toward the course, instructor, and behaviors recommended in the course) and motivation than students in control sections. Why do students develop such positive attitudes to PEP pedagogy, the course, and the instructor? One explanation is that students perceive the experience to be relevant and meaningful to them. Students in PEP section develop speeches around important social and political topics and make applications of course content to real-world contexts. They gain political knowledge by listening to their peers' speeches. In addition, they have opportunities to interact with and learn about issues confronting members of the community. One student in a PEP section of the course offered the following explanation of the relevance of this experience:

> "A main part of the semester had to do with politics. Personally, it was very beneficial to me. The persuasive speeches were very interesting and informative. It helped me gain insight on topics that I didn't know much about, like stem cell research and No Child Left Behind. Personally, I don't like to form opinions on political topics that I know nothing about.

Also, I think that since my age group is known for having low voting rates, it is important to present these political topics to us so that we realize how they affect our lives. I have found myself wanting to pay more attention to the news so I can be an educated voter."

This quote provides an example of the positive impact that educating students for democracy can have on their attitudes toward civic and political engagement as well as their behavioral intentions.

Beyond securing faculty and student support, securing funding for this work is challenging. ISU receives modest financial support from the university; however, allocated resources are not sufficient to support many of the initiatives developed over the last 10 years. As a result, ISU had to turn to external funding to support initiatives like the CER minor. This model may not be sustainable over the long term as funding priorities for foundations change. In addition, grantspersonship is time consuming and can be frustrating for faculty and staff, especially if their efforts are not met with success. As a result, those looking to expand civic and political engagement partnerships should think strategically about how they fund this work and support faculty participation.

Heartland has also experienced challenges promoting the CECS, tracking student enrollment, and communicating to those students to ensure they understand their pathway option to ISU. The sequence is comprised of general education courses that most students take with embedded civic engagement outcomes and a "capstone" course, Activism. After a few years of reviewing enrollments, Heartland learned that many students were in the activism course due to the popularity of the instructors, not because they were pursuing the sequence, such that few took advantage of the civic pathway to ISU. Recently, Heartland made some changes to embed civic engagement into its Honors Program, its Phi Theta Kappa Honors in Action project and program, and its Student Government Association leadership programming and also added the Introduction to Service-Learning course as a requirement for the sequence. This yields cohorts of students taking the courses who are easily accessible for purposes of promoting the civic pathway. We continue to work on ways to incentivize and better promote the sequence and pathway to the general student body.

Developing a comprehensive assessment plan that tracks students from one institution to the other has also proven to be challenging. At ISU, the Director of the CER Minor developed a robust assessment plan for courses in the minor. These assessment results mirror findings in the general education program discussed earlier with students in CER courses reporting significant pre- to posttest gains on a range of civic and political engagement measures. However, we have yet to develop a system for tracking students who complete the CECS at HCC and then transfer to ISU to complete the CER Minor. In the coming semesters we hope to bring stakeholders from both campuses together to develop an integrated assessment plan.

Conclusion

The argument that the civic and political disengagement of our nation's youth is a serious concern in higher education is well documented in the literature. This case study outlined a few strategies that community college and university administrators, faculty, staff, and students can employ to forge guided pathways for civic education. Although these pathways can be challenging to implement, they will continue to play a critical role in equipping the nation's students with the knowledge, skills, and motivation necessary for meaningful participation in our democracy.

Note

1. Heartland's Service-Learning and Civic Engagement webpage can be accessed at https://www.heartland.edu/service/index.html. Illinois State University's Center for Community Engagement and Service-Learning webpage can be found at https://communityengagement.illinoisstate.edu/.

References

American Association of State Colleges and Universities. (2018). American Democracy Project. Retrieved from http://www.aascu.org/programs/ADP/

Butin, D. W. (2010). *Service-learning in theory and practice: The future of community engagement in higher education.* New York, NY: Palgrave Macmillian.

Denton, R. E. (Ed.) (2017). *Political campaign communication: Theory, method, and practice.* Lanham, MD: Lexington Books.

Hillygus, D. S. (2005). The missing link: Exploring the relationship between higher education and political engagement. *Political Behavior, 27*(1), 25-47. doi:10.1007/s11109-005-3075-8.

Hunt, S., Meyer, K., Hooker, J., Simonds, C., & Lippert, L. (2016). Implementing the political engagement project in an introductory communication course: An examination of the effects on students' political knowledge, efficacy, skills, behavior, and ideology. *eJournal of Public Affairs, 5*(2), 115-120. doi:10.21768/ejopa.v5i2.111

Hunt, S. K., Simonds, C. J., & Simonds, B. K. (2009). Uniquely qualified, distinctively competent: Delivering 21st century skills in the basic course. *Basic Communication Course Annual, 21*, 1-29.

Musil, C. M. (2015). *Civic prompts: Making civic learning routine across the disciplines.* Washington, DC: Association of American Colleges and Universities.

National Task Force on Civic Learning and Democratic Engagement. (2012). *A crucible moment: College learning and democracy's future.* Washington, DC: Association of American Colleges and Universities.

Saltmarsh, J. (2005). The civic promise of service-learning. *Liberal Education, 91*(2), 50-55.

Smith, M. B., Nowacek, R. S., & Bernstein, J. L. (Eds.) (2010). *Citizenship Across the Curriculum.* Bloomington, IN: Indiana University Press.

Westheimer, J., & Kahne, J. (2004). What kind of citizen? The politics of education for democracy. *American Educational Research Journal, 41*(2), 237-269.

Woolard, C. (2017). *Engaging civic engagement: Framing the civic education movement in higher education.* Lanham, MD: Lexington Books.

Chapter 6

DEMOCRACY'S COLLEGES REVISITED

Creating an Inter-Segmental Civic Engagement Pathway between California Community Colleges and the California State Universities

Patricia D. Robinson
College of the Canyons
Santa Clarita, CA

America is a nation divided, and its democracy "flawed" (Economic Intelligence Unit Democracy Index, 2018). When examining the civic health of today's society, one finds great malaise, especially among younger generations. Polarization of political perspectives prevail while dialogue of differences falls short. These views are reflected in an alarming lack of participation, whether through voting, volunteering or joining voluntary associations, all signifiers of a healthy democracy benefiting from high rates of well-being and social capital (Finley, 2012; Putnam, 2000). Recent findings also suggest that young adults express less interest to have children, support patriotism, or believe in religion; yet, they are more inclined to favor socialism (Dann, 2019). Given the "wicked" problems (Hanstedt, 2018) of climate change, housing insecurity, and student debt that, to name only a few, greatly affect today's youth, it is no wonder that they have lost faith in democracy and envision a pessimistic, more dystopian future.

American Democracy, so relished and protected by earlier generations, appears less valued by our nation's young adults. Colleges and universities must help students to recognize their values, follow their passions; and, most importantly, to find meaning and purpose with higher education. To do this, academia must engage, empower, and encourage students to contribute to the public good--only then will participatory democracy flourish (Colby, et al., 2007).

This case study reviews the efforts of College of the Canyons (COC) to fashion a campus-wide Civic and Community Engagement Initiative capable of addressing the challenges mentioned above. The essay explores the origins of the initiative as well as its relationship to the creation of a four-year civic engagement pathway connecting with California State University, Northridge (CSUN) and its Civic and Community Engagement Minor. The essay concludes with a discussion of how the COC-CSUN partnership has expanded to include an intersegmental collaboration now working to create a civic engagement pathway model statewide.

COC and the Development of a Civic Mission

College of the Canyons (COC) is a two-year community college located in Santa Clarita, California. Situated in north Los Angeles County, it is one of 115 colleges which comprise the California Community College (CCC) system. During the 2017-18 academic year, COC served 32,862 students. Over 63 percent of these students belonged to a racial or ethnic minority group of traditionally under-represented minorities. COC is a "Hispanic serving institution, with 47 percent of its students identified as Hispanic, many of whom are first-generation (COC Fact Book, 2017-2018). These demographics reflect the majority of students attending the State's community colleges.

Although CCCs pride themselves on offering transfer and career education, they are challenged with the ever-present demand to increase student success, retention, and completion. In fact, statewide initiatives focused on Guided Pathways, equity, student success, and workforce readiness dominate the focus of campuses (see FCCC, 2017). In many cases, the California Community College Chancellor's Office has set formal benchmarks to measure success. While important, something is missing. California's Community Colleges remain silent on their original mission to emphasize civic learning and democratic engagement while articulating the social responsibility of global citizenship as "Democracy's Colleges" (Boyte, 2014). More importantly, where is the commitment of CCCs to address civic engagement, specifically by closing the "civic empowerment gap" (Levinson, 2010)? This alarming gap, argues Levinson, is as far-reaching and detrimental to students as the math and English achievement gaps that plague higher education and the workforce. Given that over 2 million students are enrolled in California's community colleges (CCCCO, 2019), campuses have an opportunity to narrow the divide affecting civic inequity.

Unfortunately, as this gap widens, rates of civic illiteracy, community engagement, and participatory democracy are also drastically plummeting. The country is witnessing a "civic recession" which is diminishing our nation's economic, political, and standing throughout the world (Campus Compact, 2010; Kanter and Schneider, 2013). The once pervasive American values to "get involved" and to "give back" have waned among the general population; and, unfortunately, Millennials are displaying some of the highest levels of apathy of any generation to date (Zukin, et al., 2006). Yet Generation Z shows a great desire to create social change (Seemiller, 2016; 2017; 2018), especially through civic and community engagement. This change is extremely important for colleges to recognize, since the earlier that individuals engage civically, the greater the likelihood that they will remain engaged throughout their lifetimes (Hollander and Burack, 2008). (See also Ehrlich, 2000; Colby et al., 2007).

With a new generation comes the opportunity to foster a "civic-minded" campus culture (*A Crucible Moment (2012)*. When placed within the context of Guided Pathways (Bailey, Jaggars, & Jenkins, 2015), California's community colleges can advance the civic engagement movement. As students commit to social, cultural, and political action, they will also increase social capital (Putnam, 2000) while strengthening American Democracy. As campuses commit to strengthen civic participation, stakeholders will recognize the importance of redefining, revising, and recapturing the interest of America's citizenry (Saltmarsh & Hartley, 2011) through "public work" (Peters, 2010). In addition, by integrating "civic prompts" (Musil, 2015) throughout California community colleges, the velocity of civic ethos, civic literacy, civic inquiry, and civic action will increase. Therefore, California Community College (CCC) and California State University (CSU) has proposed an inter-segmental Civic Engagement Pathway building on COC's Civic and Community Engagement Initiative, while working within the framework of Guided Pathways.

COC's Civic and Community Engagement Initiative: *How the Initiative Began*

In 2013-2014, Santa Clarita Community College District was awarded a *Bringing Theory to Practice Seminar Grant* entitled "Civics in Action: Recognizing College of the Canyons' Obligation to Self and Society." The grant proposal was a manifestation of the commitment of the district's Chancellor, Dr. Dianne G. Van Hook, to make civic engagement a campus-wide initiative. As the longest serving president (e.g., over 30 years) within the California Community College system, she is keenly aware of the nation's declining civic health as evidenced in *A Crucible Moment (2012)* and throughout the nationwide civic engagement movement (Campus Compact, 2010; Saltmarsh and Hartley, 2011; Scobey, 2012; Kanter & Schneider, 2013). This movement is gaining greater momentum throughout higher education, as well as at College of the Canyons, especially as a result of the publication of *A Crucible Moment (2012)* and its emphasis on the need to create "civic-minded" campus cultures.

College of the Canyons' Civic and Community Engagement Initiative originated from a day-long workshop in spring 2014 examining the concept of civic engagement. Much information was gathered from participants (e.g., students, faculty, staff, and administrators), including data collected from a campus Civic Engagement Gap Analysis and Civic Engagement S.W.O.T. Analysis. The overall results rendered valuable information, which was shared with Dr. Van Hook who immediately recognized the need to explore this topic further.

Building on this momentum, a campus team was sent to visit De Anza College in Northern California which houses the Vasconcellos Institute for Democracy in Action. De Anza College was a logical starting point, given its long and accomplished history of addressing civic and community engagement. The COC team met with students, staff, and then president, Dr. Brian Murphy. A report of the visit was presented to the Chancellor, as well as a concept paper suggesting the plan to create a campus-wide civic engagement initiative. By spring 2015, Chancellor Van Hook conceptualized the merits of establishing a new Center for Civic Engagement.

Wasting little time, a group of faculty quickly convened with the author in late spring 2015 to frame the emerging initiative. Professors from English, Anthropology, Sociology, Communication Studies, and Political Science all agreed that Thomas Ehrlich's definition best captured what COC envisioned for civic engagement, stating, it is about *"working to make a difference in the civic life of our communities and developing the combination of knowledge, skills, values and motivation to make that difference. It means promoting the quality of life in a community, through both political and non-political processes"* (Ehrlich, 2000, p. vi). His words continue to guide the work of civic and community engagement at College of the Canyons.

Next steps included developing a strategic plan. The author conducted an extensive literature review, combed websites, and examined two- and four-year college and university civic engagement departments and programs. *A Call to Action: An Initiative for Civic Engagement, Self, and Society*, was written and submitted to Chancellor Van Hook on August 1, 2015, the official start date of the position. The initiative, following closely the tenets of *A Crucible Moment (2012)*, emphasizes the need to infuse aspects of civic engagement throughout the campus milieu. "If civic engagement is to gain real traction in today's higher education," suggests Barbara Jacoby, "it must be clearly defined, and civic learning outcomes must be established." In other words, "Opportunities to learn about and practice civic engagement must be embedded throughout the curriculum and co-curriculum" (Jacoby, 2009, p. 2). Only then can a civic-minded culture truly exist.

Three weeks later, a multidisciplinary Civic Engagement Steering Committee formed, which remains strong today. Comprised of administrators, faculty, staff, students, and community partner voices, the Committee prevails as the driving force behind the initiative. Members work to break down campus silos and to bridge theory with practice (e.g., praxis) while fostering representative thought and dialogue to enhance the public good. Through collaboration, reciprocity, and action, the Committee encourages civic and community engagement, as it brings awareness of issues affecting the well-being of self and society (Astin & Sax, 1998; Astin, Sax, & Avalos, 1999; Thoits & Hewitt, 2001; Uslaner 2002). In addition, the core values of equity, activism, dignity, leadership, integrity, and mutual respect permeate throughout the initiative, as well as the work of the Center for Civic Engagement.

The initiative has grown extensively in its less than four years of existence. Recognizing networking opportunities and building collaborative partnerships is an integral part of civic engagement work, and the Center has developed relationships and shared programming with many diverse groups , including The Democracy Commitment, Campus Compact, the Kettering Foundation, California Campus Compact, Association of American Colleges and Universities, Bringing Theory to Practice, Civic

Learning and Democratic Engagement (CLDE), Imagining America, Foundation for California Community Colleges, Academic Senate for California Community Colleges, Young Invincibles, #VoteTogether, ALL IN Campus Democracy Challenge, Zonta, League of Women Voters of the Santa Clarita Valley, Band of Voters, RP Group (Research, Planning, Professional Development for California Community Colleges), 3CSN (California Community Colleges Success Networking, National Society of Leadership and Success), and, most recently, Stanford University's Haas Center for Public Service.

Activities related to these organizations have included Deliberative Dialogue training from the Kettering Foundation, topics presented at multiple regional and national conferences, and leadership opportunities through Campus Compact and NSLS. In addition, funding from AAC&U and Bringing Theory to Practice for multiple projects, including Department by Design, Multi-Institution Innovation Projects and Amplifying, Dissemination, and Increasing the Public Reach of Research and Practice grants. Engage the Election support assisted the campus in promoting a large mid-term election "get out the vote" campaign, as well as brought greater attention to voter education, awareness, and engagement. Through the FCCC's Civic Impact Project, four civic scholars created a semester-length project and were recognized by the Foundation in Sacramento, California. This semester, three students are participating in the national 2019 Imaging America Gathering, while two others are serving as California Campus Compact Community Engagement Student Fellows.

Getting Started: Creating a Local Civic Engagement Pathway with College of the Canyons and California State University, Northridge

The first objective addressed by the new director was to meet with representatives from COC's primary four-year transfer institutions; specifically, California State University, Northridge (CSUN) and University of California, Los Angeles (UCLA). In each case, both institutions offer civic and community engagement minors and incorporate community engagement through Service-Learning; or, what many colleges and universities are now calling Community-Based Learning. In reviewing course requirements for the minors, it was apparent that CSUN's lower-division classes could articulate with courses found within the California Community College system. However, coursework required of the UCLA minor was unique to the University of California system only.

Meeting with CSUN's Director of Community Engagement, Director of Civic and Community Engagement Program, and faculty working directly with the minor, the idea of how to create a Civic and Community Engagement (CCE) pathway for students transferring to CSUN quickly transpired. Discussion focused on how COC could create a fifteen-unit *Civic Engagement Certificate of Specialization* which would, upon transfer, fulfill nine of the required eighteen units of CSUN's Civic and Community Engagement Minor. Given that 878 COC students transferred to CSU fall semester 2018; and, out of that number, 70 percent enrolled at CSUN, this certificate will address each of the four pillars of Guided Pathways (California State University, 2018). To ensure that students both clarify and enter the civic and community engagement pathway during their first semester, work is taking place with the local high school district to expand the proposed 4 + 2 model to a 4 + 2 + 2 model. This is a strategic move, since 60 percent of students from the William S. Hart High School District transfer to COC (COC Fact Book, 2017-2018).

The power of the civic and community pathway rests in the effort to identify what drives students with regard to meaningful and purposeful work. The earlier that students recognize their passion, the sooner they engage in selecting a major which will lead them to finding a "role for their soul" (Pearce, 2019, p. xi). This is especially true for the younger workforce, since "graduates with high purpose in work are almost 10 times more likely to have high overall wellbeing" (Gallup, 2019, p. 7). Today's students want to commit to the betterment of society, especially through their support of social causes (Seemiller, 2018). As we work to engage students early in civic engagement opportunities, especially through aspects of Integrative Learning (Huber and Hutchings, 2004), a "civic-mindset" is being developed. Creating "wicked students" to examine "wicked problems" (Hanstedt, 2018) incorporating Growth Mindset (Dweck, 2007), Critical Community-Based Learning (Mitchell, 2007; 2008), Project Based Learning (Wobbe & Stoddard, 2019), as well as Design Thinking (Lewrick, et al., 2008) and Action Research (Stringer, 2007), moves the focus of engagement from hours to impact. Strengthening integrative learning experiences, including Community-Based Learning, Project-Based Learning, and internships, will addresses all four pillars of Guided Pathways while helping students make connections and find relevancy to local, national, and global concerns.

This emerging pathway model seeks to provide students with "real world" opportunities in which they can expand on their individual interests, talents, and abilities throughout their college years. It also emphasizes the 21st Century professional skills of creativity, collaboration, critical thinking, and communication—qualities employers seek in today's workforce (Hart, 2018). In addition, it is a holistic, scaffold approach which integrates aspects of "public work" throughout all disciplines, as well as co-curricular activities (Peters, 2010). It also argues that all students, not only those involved in honors, clubs or student government, get involved. If the community college is going to close the equity gap, increase student success, and bridge campus with community, it must involve the work of all students, no matter their assessment measures, financial placements or discipline interests. The sooner students connect to their community, whether on- or off-campus, the more likely they will remain invested in it. Because most students remain in their local communities, it is important to foster a sense of civic stewardship and community well-being among students during their first semester.

In designing the Civic Engagement Certificate of Specialization, the author reframed CSUN's minor's lower-division General Education (GE) Paths of Arts, Media, and Culture; Global Studies; Principles of Sustainability; Health and Wellness; and Social Justice to include subject clusters most related to classes offered at COC, including 1) Gender, Sexuality, and Diversity, 2) Culture, Race, and Ethnicity, 3) Ethics, Law, and Communication, and 4) Inequality, Equity, and Critical Thinking. Within these clusters, students choose from over 50 electives selected from 16 disciplines.

Most students can complete the certificate, since all electives include GE breadth requirements. In addition, two new courses were written for the certificate: *Introduction to Community-Based Learning* and *Introduction to Civic and Community Engagement*. The second course articulates with CSUN's comparable lower-division course of Introduction to Civic and Community Engagement. CSUN does not currently offer an equivalent lower-division CBL course. These courses are pending approval from the California Community College Chancellor's Office.

A large percentage of students who transfer from COC to CSUN declare majors closely associated with civic and community engagement. This includes those fulfilling requirements for Associate of Transfer Degrees (ATDs) in Sociology, Communication Studies, Social Justice or Political Science, as well as students completing units for the Pathway to Law School. While the civic and community engagement pathway is in its infancy, the long-term goal is to create a seamless articulation and transfer process for COC. Although this objective is a natural fit for many disciplines within the social sciences, it also provides an opportunity to advance civic and community engagement throughout the Arts, STEM, Humanities, and Career Education. No matter the field of study, "Democracy's Colleges" have an obligation to instill the foundations of civic and community "stewardship" (Ronan 2011, p. 5) throughout the next generation of global citizens.

Scaling Up: Building an Intersegmental Civic Engagement Pathway between California Community Colleges and California State Universities

The California Community College system, as previously mentioned, includes 115 colleges and 72 community college districts. The system serves over 2.1 million students, the majority of whom are first generation and students of color. The majority of community college students who transfer to a 4-year institution tend to stay in-state and continue their studies at California State University. The California State University is a public university system with 23 campuses and eight off-campus centers enrolling 484,300 students with 26,858 faculty and 25,305 staff. While enrollments are high, years to transfer and graduation, as well as overall success and completion rates, are more concerning. With strong integrative, inter-segmental partnerships, institutions can provide strategic alignment between majors, programs, and degrees (e.g., Associate Transfer Degree) to increase student success. (See CCCCO, 2019; CSUOC, 2019).

CCC and CSU represent the two largest public systems of higher education in the country and two of the largest found in the world. Combined, California State University and California's community colleges serve the majority of the nation's undergraduates. The time is right to create an inter-segmental Civic Engagement Pathway. If executed with a solid plan of action, the resulting civic outcomes related to literary, skills, and action will be impressive throughout the classroom, campus, and community. In short, it is time to move the discussion of civic engagement on campuses from margin to center and hopefully expand traditional definitions of student engagement (See Pollack, 2011; Pollack & Motoike, 2005; Bowen, 2010; Smith, Nowacek, & Bernstein, 2010; Butin & Seider, 2012; and Campus Compact, 2010, 2012.)

The initial idea to design a civic and community engagement pathway between CSU Northridge and College of the Canyons has expanded to create an inter-segmental collaboratory between the California State University and California Community College systems. The ultimate goal is to develop a replicable inter-segmental model two and four-year campuses statewide. The initial details of such a plan are being worked out by a group representing the first-ever California Community College and California State University Civic Engagement Coalition. Comprised of representatives from the CSU and CCC systems, as well as statewide non-profit partners from 3CSN and California Career Ladders, the group is moving forward to establish a civic engagement pathway between California's higher education systems.

Concurrent with the establishment of the coalition, two relevant proposals stressing the importance of curricular collaboration and professional development training across systems, have recently been awarded Bringing Theory to Practice *Now is the Time to Create a Crucible Moment: Addressing the Civic Empowerment Gap Among California's Community Colleges* grants.

The first proposal, *Creating a Crucible Moment: Building an Integrative Civic Engagement Pathway Between California's Post-Secondary System*, emphasizes two separate inter-segmental partnerships, one between Cerritos College and CSU Dominguez Hills and the second between CSUN and College of the Canyons. Campuses will bring faculty together to redesign General Education curriculum that will intentionally incorporate active and integrative learning opportunities with a focus on civic engagement. (COC will also examine Career Education curriculum.) This project will develop a more cohesive, integrative learning experience for students starting at the community college and transferring to the university. It will also directly support the implementation of Guided Pathways at Cerritos College and College of the Canyons and provide for a better alignment between transferable California State University General Education (CSUGE) options within selected Program Road Maps at CSUDH and CSUN. In addition, the project will specifically support the work of the RP Group for California Community Colleges and its "crosswalk" of Student Support and Guided Pathways (see RP Group, 2017). This work will help meet these goals.

The second proposal, entitled *Now is the Time to Create a Crucible Moment: Addressing the Civic Empowerment Gap Among California's Community Colleges*, similarly addresses the need for inter-segmental dialogue and instruction in the area of civic engagement and

Community-Based Learning between two- and four-year colleges and universities in California. Professional development training will incorporate the opportunities, challenges, outcomes, and lessons learned thus far in creating a "civic-minded" campus culture at College of the Canyons, CSU Los Angeles, and the University of La Verne; and, in turn, in their respective communities (*A Crucible Moment*, 2012). Workshops will bring together civic engagement representatives from the CSU-5 (e.g., CSU Northridge, CSU Dominguez Hills, CSU Los Angeles, CSU Long Beach, and California State Polytechnic University, Pomona), along with Community Engagement staff from the University of La Verne. In addition, given the location of these 4-year institutions within the Los Angeles Basin and their 52 community college partner institutions, faculty from two-year campuses will play an important role in this collaboration. In fact, training will inform participants of the "civic empowerment gap" (Levinson, 2010) and provide examples of how to confront the problem by creating individualized civic engagement initiatives; or, more specifically, civic action plans. Combined outcomes from these two projects will help to build a California inter-segmental community of practice model.

Civic Engagement Initiative Challenges

Despite strong momentum across the state, and specific administrative and financial support to develop, facilitate, and implement a new civic engagement initiative at College of the Canyons, challenges remain. The most significant challenge has involved the concept of disciplinary "territory" or "turf." At no other time at COC had the concept of civic engagement been discussed or placed within a larger definition, as suggested by Ehrlich (2000). In other words, all things "civic" have historically been relegated to specific disciplines, especially history and political science. As a result, the notion of civic has primarily been defined in terms of history, politics, and government only, not the larger context of public work, social responsibility, and community engagement. Civic Engagement is applicable to all disciplines, whether transfer or career education. As a result, some departments, disciplines, and programs, whether intentional or unintentional, remain less integrative to the work of the Center for Civic Engagement.

Faculty engagement or "buy in" has been another challenge. Ironically, many faculty are currently embedding aspects of civic and community engagement throughout their courses; however, recognizing the connection to the initiative has met with some resistance. It is not because individuals are opposed to the premise of civic and community engagement, but some see the initiative as part of a larger directive. As previously mentioned, faculty are experiencing "initiative overload," especially as more and more mandates are being sent forward from the California Community College Chancellor's Office. Faculty are being asked to do more with less, and, unfortunately, they must prioritize their time and energy. This translates to limited time to participate in multiple initiatives, resulting in faculty support from afar only. There also exists for others the question of how civic engagement connects to their disciplines, much less their individual courses. This has especially been the case with Community-Based Learning serving as the primary pedagogical vehicle of Civic Engagement. Many faculty believe that civic and community work relate primarily to the social sciences, not to the humanities, fine arts or sciences; and, in most cases, they are unable to make connections or recognize the relevancy to social issues. Again, most think of civic engagement only in terms of history, politics or government, not within the larger context of addressing issues from a transdisciplinary approach.

In addition, evaluation and assessment measures are currently lacking, as are overall student learning outcomes. However, multiple AAC&U VALUE Rubrics are under review, including those for Civic Engagement, Integrative Learning, and Global Learning (see aacu.org). While the Civic Engagement Steering Committee works to construct an evaluation tool which will accurately measure the impact of civic engagement and its related activities, it continues to administer qualitative measures.

Additional challenges existed with securing office space and furniture. This task was quickly remedied by identifying a large underutilized storage area and securing surplus furniture. Next, there was the challenge of who was the faculty director to report to, as the Center for Civic Engagement established roots in Academic Affairs. Only once Community-Based Learning (formally called Service-Learning) was absorbed by the Center for Civic Engagement that the initiative was moved under the supervision of the Dean of Integrative Learning and Career Education. This realignment was instrumental, since the dean serves as a champion of the Center and its work. If a champion is absent; or, if a supervisor fails to feel the passion or share the vision for social change with the director, then moving forward will meet resistance.

Lastly, while innovation funds supported the Center's first year, these funds did not exist the following year and funding was dependent on outside sources, especially grants. As a result, grant writing has become an important component of the faculty director's position. In addition, administrative assistance was no longer available after the first year; and, to date, the Center operates with no formal support staff. Permanent funding was reinstituted by year three and is formally recognized in the Center's annual program review. Commitment to ongoing financial support has resulted in the first step of institutionalizing the program, as well as ensuring sustainability. In addition, with the recent absorption of the former service-learning program, a 72 percent classified coordinator position is being rewritten to 100 percent and reflects the needs of the Center.

The Impact of the Civic Engagement Initiative

The impact of COC's Civic Engagement Initiative rests primarily on qualitative responses, since structured evaluation tools do not currently exist. This will change over the next year as structured assessment measures develop. Since the inception of the initiative, the Center for Civic Engagement has brought a variety of speakers to campus, ranging from campus-wide presentations and deliberative dialogues to faculty workshops to student panel discussions. Topics of discussion have examined human trafficking, sexual harassment and assault, homelessness, veterans issues, inmate education, DACA (Deferred Action for Childhood Arrivals), free speech, voter suppression, and civility. In some cases, attendance has exceeded 200 participants. College of the Canyons has also hosted two state-wide California Community College Civic Engagement Summits. The Center has also welcomed outside experts to provide training in civic engagement, Community-Based Learning, civility, deliberative dialogue, conflict resolution, and peace studies. In addition, the Center works closely with the Office of Student Development and the Associated Student Government to support student engagement. Additional ways that the initiative is impacting the campus, as previously mentioned, is through various grants and collaborations that the Center has established with many groups.

Quantitative data do exist, however, with regard to COC's first-time, dedicated effort to increase voter registration and participation. Working with Engage the Vote though Campus Compact's Democracy Commitment Initiative for Community Colleges, along with Tufts

University's National Study of Learning, Voting, and Engagement (NSLVE) Initiative, Civic Nation, #VoteTogether, and All-In Campus Democracy Challenge, COC has done much this semester to create a "civic mind-set" focused on political engagement. In fact, when realizing that of 12,944 of COC's eligible student voters, only 1,636 actually voted; or, stated differently, only 12.6 percent of students cast a ballot during the 2014 midterm election—much work is needed. Interestingly, 6,935 students at COC registered for the first time in 2014 while 53.6 percent voted. However, of those who voted, only 23.6 percent were between the ages of 18-24, the age group whose voice is most lacking at the polls. NSLVE data clearly show that COC's action plan must also attend to voter education and participation year-round, not solely during voter registration cycles (NSLVE, 2018).

COC currently holds a bronze seal in comparison with 844 colleges and universities nationwide that are involved in Civic Nation's All-In Campus Democracy Challenge (see All-In Challenge Homepage). Through the efforts of many campus members this semester, we hope to increase COC student voter registration for the 2018 midterm election by 10 percent (e.g., 691 students) and voter participation by 10 percent (e.g. 164 students). In addition, campus political engagement goals are now set for the next two years. Lastly, Band of Voters, working with Young Invincibles, worked to author California Assembly Bill 963 (AB 963), *Student Civic and Voter Empowerment Act—California Public Universities*. The bill was introduced by Assembly member Cottie Petrie-Norris, 74th Assembly District, on April 26, 2019, to the California State Assembly Higher Education Sub-committee. College of the Canyons provided testimony in support of the bill, which passed is now moving forward in the legislative approval process. Finally, the Center is working with the Office of the Los Angeles County Registrar-Recorder/County Clerk to make COC a Mega-Vote Center for the upcoming 2020 elections.

Conclusion

Creating an integrative, holistic civic and community engagement inter-segmental pathway between the California Community College and California State University systems will yield impressive results. First, students who take abstract concepts and apply them to real-world events will comprehend material better, as well as retain greater knowledge. Second, students will learn higher order thinking skills like critical thinking, writing, and communication. Third, students will increase their emotional intelligence, making them more aware of their environments, as well as the diverse groups around them. Fourth, as levels of civic literacy swell, so will participation in civic engagement. Finally, as students apply theory to practice (e.g., praxis) and experience social conditions firsthand (or study a social issue in depth), they will learn to conceptualize, synthesize, and analyze social groups, problems, and outcomes with a greater degree of knowledge, understanding, and empathy. As a result, their enhanced civic development will lead to greater civic maturity which results in an informed and engaged citizenry. (See Cress, 2012; Checkoway, 2014, 2015). By placing the concept of a "civic-minded" campus culture (*A Crucible Moment, 2012*) within the larger context of Guided Pathways and inter-segmental collaborations, California's community colleges can advance the "civic engagement movement." As students join together for change, they are also increasing social capital while strengthening American Democracy.

To ensure that students both clarify and enter the civic and community engagement pathway during their first semester, work is taking place with the local high school district to expand the proposed civic engagement pathway to include juniors and seniors, many of whom (e.g., 60 percent) will transfer from the William S. Hart High School District to COC (COC Fact Book, 2017-2018). The earlier we can get students involved in the pathway, the better we can ensure completion of Civic Engagement Certificate requirements and successful transfer to CSUN.

References

ALL-IN Campus Democracy Challenge. (2019). Washington, D.C. See allinchallenge.org.

Astin, A. W. & Sax L. J. (1998). How undergraduates are affected by service participation. *Journal of College Student Development, 39*(93), 251-63.

Astin, A. W., Sax, L. J., & Avalos, J. (1999). The long-term effects of volunteerism during the undergraduate years." *Review of Higher Education 21*(2), 187-202.

Association of American Colleges and Universities [AACU]. (2019). Washington, D.C. See aacu.org.

Bailey, T., Jaggars, S., & Jenkins, D. (2015). *Redesigning America's community colleges: A clearer path to student success.* Cambridge, MA: Harvard University Press

Bowen, G. (2010). *Civic Engagement in Higher Education: Resources and References*. Cullowhee, NC: Center for Service-learning at Western Carolina University.

Boyte, H. C. (2014). *Democracy's education: Public work, citizenship, and the future of colleges and universities.* Nashville, TN: Vanderbilt University Press.

California Community Colleges Chancellor's Office (CCCCO). 2019. *Datamart.* See https://datamart.cccco.edu/.

California State University Chancellor's Office (2018). *CSU Graduation Initiative 2025 Update*. Long Beach, CA: California State University Chancellor's Office.

California State University. (2018). *Institutional Research and Analyses*. See http://www.calstate.edu/as/. Specific data for College of the Canyons is found in Table 3, https://www.calstate.edu/as/stat_reports/2018-2019/fc-cct03.htm.

Campus Compact. (2012). *A praxis brief: Campus Compact's response to* A crucible moment: College learning and democracy's future. Boston, MA: Campus Compact.

Campus Compact. (2010). *A promising connection: Increasing college access and success through civic engagement.* Boston, MA: Campus Compact.

Cerritos College Homepage. (2019). See www.cerittos.edu.

Checkoway, B. (2014). The connection between civic engagement and well-being. *A Bringing Theory to Practice Well-Being Seminar,* November 6-7, 2014. Washington, D.C.: Association of American Colleges and Universities, p. 18.

Colby, A., Beaumont, E., Ehrlich, T., & Corngold, J. (2007). *Preparing undergraduates for responsible political engagement.* San Francisco, CA: Jossey-Bass.

Colby, A., Ehrlich, T., Beaumont, E. & Stephens, J. (2007). *Educating citizens: Preparing America's undergraduates for lives of moral and civic responsibility.* San Francisco, CA: Jossey-Bass.

College of the Canyons. (2017-2018). *College of the Canyons Fact Book*. Santa Clarita, CA: College of the Canyons.

Dann, C. (2019). "A deep and boiling anger": NBC/WSJ poll finds a pessimistic American despite current economic satisfaction. Retrieved from https://www.nbcnews.com/politics/meet-the-press/deep-boiling-anger-nbc-wsj-poll-finds-pessimistic-america-despite-n1045916.

Dweck, C. S. (2007). *Mindset: The new psychology of success.* New York, NY: Ballentine Books.

Ehrlich, T. [Ed]. (2000). *Civic responsibility and higher education.* Phoenix, AZ: Oryx Press.

Feminist Newswire. (2019, October 9). Groundbreaking student voter bill signed into law in California. Retrieved from https://msmagazine.com/2019/10/09/groundbreaking-student-voter-bill-signed-into-law-in-california/.

Finley, A. (2012). The joy of learning: The impact of civic engagement on psychosocial well-being." *Diversity and Democracy 15*(3), 8-9.

Foundation for California Community Colleges. (2017). *Vision for success: Strengthening the California community colleges to meet California's needs.* Sacramento, CA: Foundation for California Community Colleges.

Gallup. (2019). *Forging pathways to purposeful work: The role of higher education.* Washington, D.C.: Gallup World Headquarters.

Hanstedt, P. (2018). *Creating wicked students: Designing courses for a complex world.* Sterling, VA: Stylus Publishing.

Hart Research Associates. (2018). *"Fulfilling the American Dream: Liberal education and the future of work: Selected findings from online surveys of business executives and hiring managers."* Washington, D.C.: Association of American Colleges and Universities.

Hollander, E. & Burack, C. (2008). *How young people develop long-lasting habits of civic engagement: A conversation on building a research agenda.* Spencer Foundation, June 24-26, 2008.

Huber, M. T. & Hutchings, P. (2004). *Integrative learning: Mapping the terrain.* Washington, D.C.: Association of American Colleges and Universities.

Jacoby, B. & Associates. (2009). *Civic engagement in higher education: Concepts and practices.* New York, NY: Wiley and Sons.

Kanter, M. & Schneider, C. G. (2013). Civic learning and engagement. *Change: The Magazine of Higher Learning.* January-February.

Levinson, M. (2010). The civic empowerment gap: Defining the problem and locating solutions." In L. Sherrod, L., J. Torney-Purta, & C. A. Flanagan (Eds.), *Handbook of research on civic engagement* (pp. 331-361). Hoboken, NJ: John Wiley & Sons.

Lewrick, M., Link, P., & Leifer, L. (2018). *The design thinking playbook: Mindful digital transformation of teams, products, services, businesses and ecosystems.* Hoboken, NY: John Wiley & Sons.

Mills, C. W. (2000) [1959]. *The sociological imagination*. 40th Anniversary Edition. Oxford, UK: Oxford University Press.

Mitchell, T. D. (2007). Critical service-learning as social justice education: A case study of the Citizen Scholars Program. *Equity and Excellence in Education 40*, 101-112.

Mitchell, T. D. (2008). "Traditional vs. Critical Service-Learning: Engaging the literature to differentiate two models." *Michigan Journal of Community Service-learning*, Spring 2008, 50-65.

Musil, C. M. (2015). *Civic prompts: Making civic learning routine across the disciplines*. Washington, D.C.: Association for American Colleges and Universities.

National Task Force on Civic Learning and Democratic Engagement. (2012). *A crucible moment: College learning and democracy's future*. Washington, D.C.: American Colleges and Universities.

Pearce, N. (2019). *The purpose path: A guide to pursuing your authentic life's work*. New York, NY: St. Martin's Essentials.

Peters, S. J. (2010). *Democracy in higher education: Traditions and stories of civic engagement*. Transformations in Higher Education series. Ann Arbor, MI: Michigan State University Press.

Pollack, S. & Motoike, P. (2006). Civic engagement through service-learning at CSU Monterey Bay: Educating multicultural community builders." *Metropolitan Universities: Indicators of Engagement 17*(1), 36-50.

Pollack, S. (2011). Civic literacy across the curriculum. *Diversity and Democracy 14*(3): 1-3.

Putnam, R. D. (2002). *Bowling alone: The collapse and revival of American community*. New York, NY: Simon and Schuster.

RP Group. (2017). *Crosswalk: Where student support (RE)defined and Guided Pathways meet: Using the success factors to facilitate pathways planning*. Sacramento, CA: RP Group.

Robinson, P. (2015). *A call to action: An initiative for civic engagement for self and society*. Santa Clarita, CA: College of the Canyons.

Ronan, B. (2012). Community colleges and the work of democracy. Connections: *The Kettering Foundation's Annual Newsletter*. Dayton, OH: Kettering Foundation. Spring Issue: 31-33.

Ronan, B. (2011). *The civic spectrum: How students become engaged citizens*. Dayton, OH: Kettering Foundation.

Saltmarsh, J. & Hartley, M. [Eds.]. (2011). *"To serve a larger purpose": Engagement for democracy and the transformation of higher education.* Philadelphia: PA: Temple University Press.

Scobey, D. M. (2012). A Copernican moment: On the revolutions in higher education. In D. W. Harward (Ed.), *Transforming undergraduate education: Theory that compels and practices that succeed* (pp. 37-50). New York, NY: Rowman and Littlefield.

Seemiller, C. & Grace, M. (2018). *Generation Z: A century in the making.* New York, NY: Routledge Press.

Seemiller, C. & Grace, M. (2017). *Generation Z leads: A guide for developing the leadership capacity of Generation Z students.* North Charleston, SC: CreateSpace Independent Publishing Platform.

Seemiller, C. & Grace, M. (2016). *Generation Z goes to college.* San Francisco, CA: Jossey-Bass.

Smith, M. B., Nowacek, R. S., & Bernstein, J. L. (Eds.) (2010). *Citizenship across the curriculum.* Bloomington, IN: Indiana University Press.

Stringer, E. T. (2007). *Action research.* Third edition. Thousand Oaks, CA: SAGE Publications.

The Economist Intelligence Unit. (2018). *Democracy Index 2018: Me too? Political participation, protest, and democracy.* New York, NY: The Economist.

Thoits, P.A. & L. N. Hewitt. (2001). Volunteer work and well-being." *Journal of Health and Social Behavior 42*(June), 115-31.

Uslaner, E.M. (2002). *The Moral foundation of trust.* New York, NY: Cambridge University Press.

Wobbe, K, and Stoddard, E.A. (2019). *Project-based learning in the First Year.* Sterling, VA: Stylus Publishing.

Zukin, C., Keeter, S., Andolina, M., Jenkins, K., & Delli Carpini, M. X. (2006). *A new engagement: Political participation, civic life, and the changing American citizen.* New York, NY: Oxford University Press.

Chapter 7

CHANGE OF PERSPECTIVE

Finding your Community Engagement Fit to Put Students First

Erin Riney
Durham Technical Community College
Durham, North Carolina

Durham Technical Community College is situated in one of the most highly educated areas of the United States. Not only does a large percentage of the area's residents hold advanced degrees, but the Triangle region (Raleigh, Durham, and Chapel Hill areas) also draws thousands of students to three major research universities, seven other private or public universities, and two community colleges, including the largest community college in the state. Home to GlaxoSmithKline's largest research and development center, IBM's second largest operation in the world, the National Institute of Environmental Health Science, and a hub for hundreds of tech and life science companies, the number of colleges and educated professionals has led to the area being called the land of "Trees, trees, and Ph.D.s" (Kroll, 2014).

An awareness of this robust, asset-rich educational and economic context, however, would likely elude a visitor to our community college. Our main campus is situated between an urban industrial zone and one of the area's largest and oldest public housing developments. On one side of our campus, fifty-eight percent of our neighborhood's residents live below the poverty line. Other areas abutting the main campus have been identified as the most impoverished in the city, with residents' bachelor's degree attainment numbering in the single digits.

In 2011, our college president named our college's 50th anniversary a "Year of Service." Among other activities, we established a series of one-time employee volunteer opportunities, an employee Community Engagement Award, a mechanism for tracking volunteer hours, and our first community partnerships. After that anniversary year, we looked to shift focus to student engagement and build a true culture of service on campus.

When we began developing our student-focused community engagement efforts, we turned for guidance to our nearby 4-year colleges and universities and their well-established community engagement offices. Their extensive community partnerships, well-integrated and supported service-learning courses, and comprehensive volunteer and student leadership opportunities were inspirational. Their faculty and staff welcomed us and supported our interest in service-learning and civic engagement, sharing resources and inviting us to their professional development and speaker events. However, while our campus is fewer than 5 miles from Duke University, and only about 20 from UNC-Chapel Hill and NC State University, our student populations and institutional resources could not be further apart. Our students pay $1,986 per year; Duke's pay $55,695. UNC-Chapel Hill has an annual operating budget of $3 billion; ours is $52 million. NC State's average student is full-time, male, white, and 18-22. Our average student is part-time, female, Black Non-Hispanic, and 24 or older. Even among our area community colleges, we were comparing apples and oranges due to size and funding differences.

A Change of Approach

Initially, it seemed our challenge was to find a way to either resize our neighboring campuses' activities to fit our college or address our college's deficits within existing community engagement models. As we looked at great examples of volunteer engagement, service-learning courses, learning communities, or volunteer trips abroad at area 4-year institutions, we could not replicate those activities. We have no sororities or fraternities to engage in service competitions, no funding for instructor stipends or course releases to redesign syllabi, no dorms for living-learning communities, and no budgets or staff for out-of-state Alternative Service Breaks, much less volunteer trips abroad, which our students wouldn't even be able to afford. Everywhere we looked, we saw what we lacked to be able to replicate 4-year schools' models of civic engagement.

We often heard the recommendation or read of great programs that utilized student leaders to establish community partnerships, run tutoring programs, or plan and lead service breaks. However, the reality of our community college is that our students are working—often multiple jobs—and carrying many responsibilities in their lives. Even when we found students who had the time to engage on such a level, they often transferred not long after we identified their talent and began to train them. Or oftentimes their social and financial safety nets weren't enough to allow them to continue their civic engagement interests when life setbacks happened. For example, we invested significant staff time in selecting and supporting several students in two different part-time AmeriCorps programs, only to have zero students complete their service and receive their educational award. Students had to drop these long-term commitments when they lost their transportation in a wreck or needed to work additional paying hours to support their families. When we tried utilizing student leaders in place of staff for off-campus volunteer events, we lost community partnerships because we hadn't realized the amount of training those leaders needed, especially around professionalism. Many of our students are first-generation college students and don't know some of the unstated but still expected behaviors of office settings or professional interactions, things many students from more affluent socio-economic statuses absorb without trying. That's one of the very reasons civic engagement opportunities can be so beneficial for our students, providing them with that exposure or training and building their professional networks. We just needed a way to scaffold those experiences and meet our students where they are.

After some false starts, dead ends, and even negative experiences, we eventually realized the problems we were encountering weren't a result of our funding, specific student population, or size. The problem was using more resource-rich, traditional 4-year colleges' examples of community engagement as our yardstick. Our successes came after we switched our perspective from a deficit- to asset-based approach for designing and implementing community engagement. Focusing on our assets does not mean we ignore the very real challenges that we and other community colleges face in developing strong community engagement offices, such as our status as a commuter campus, students' extensive work and family responsibilities, transportation constraints, extensive barriers to staffing and funding, lack of buy-in from key administrators, the fact that we serve predominantly low- to no-income students (and the list goes on). Instead, by recognizing how we are uniquely positioned to engage with our local communities allowed us to see obstacles as hurdles, not barriers, and to create our own community engagement standards and priorities for our college and our students. We've crafted an approach that works for us and has allowed positive benefits for our college, community, and students while still following the spirit, if not best practices, of community engagement work.

Lessons Learned

Many of the assets we leveraged are not unique to our specific community college. Certainly, some community colleges will not identify with all of the situations we face, due to variation in institutional support, location, or student populations. However, we hope many community colleges that either feel distanced by metrics or best practices that appear unrealistic for their colleges, feel unacknowledged for their hard-fought successes because they aren't similar to program examples lifted up by the field, or don't typically find themselves represented in community engagement conversations will find the following strategies helpful and reflective of the realities of their campuses and students' experiences.

One: Our smaller size means less bureaucracy and the ability to be more nimble in how we navigate the design and implementation of community engagement initiatives.

As a community college with about 5,500 FTE students, we are large enough to have name recognition in the community and a sizeable pool of students to engage, but small enough to avoid time-consuming red tape to establish new initiatives. Also, since we are not a large university, we are more familiar with our coworkers and can identify key faculty or staff who may support our efforts or who themselves may be eager to engage in the community. My office is down the hall from the dean of our university transfer program, and our hallway conversations lead to the inclusion of service-learning in upcoming job advertisements for instructor positions. Our quick hallway chats accomplish the same result that a larger school would need a committee, several meetings, and likely a formal recommendation from the Chief Academic Officer to achieve.

Our students often bring greater awareness and understanding—if not experience—to their community engagement activities, an advanced acumen that fosters meaningful engagement and contributions to their communities. Although students at 4-year institutions most certainly face life challenges, research consistently shows that community colleges enroll more first-generation, low-income, minority, and adult students (Ma and Baum, 2016). Due to this variation in student characteristics at 4-year and 2-year public colleges, community college students on the whole are less likely to be "voluntourists" dabbling in an afternoon or weekend of seeing "how the other half lives." When our students engage in their communities, their eyes are most often already open to the realities of disparity because they are living those inequalities of race, socio-economic status, age, ability, health care, food security, housing security, and more.

For example, a student group preparing enrichment activities for children at a local public housing development gained insight from a fellow student volunteer who had grown up in the apartments. In another case, students' post-service reflections during our homeless shelter dinner shift was enriched and informed by a fellow student volunteer who previously had been a shelter resident. While our students may need assistance to more fully understand systemic or institutional causes of inequalities, their lived experiences often afford them greater insight into and empathy for complications and barriers affecting our community and our community partners' clients.

Two: Our students are motivated by their desire to contribute.

Community college students' familiarity with social inequalities also engenders a passion for change and a motivation to be of use. I have heard counterparts at 4-year universities lament their students' drive to start non-profits to advance their candidacy for graduate school or specific careers without conversations with the affected population, investigation into community need, or acknowledgement of possible duplication of existing efforts. It is rare for our students to think first of how service work can serve them. More often our students are motivated by empathy, compassion, and a desire to make a difference rather than to get ahead or build a resume. When presenting optional service-learning projects or recruiting volunteers for service events, appealing to this motivation can increase participation. For example, for our Associate in Applied Science certificate program in Spanish Interpretation, enrolled students are given the option to attend conferences or to participate in service-learning. The majority of these students, who have often witnessed or experienced the challenges of language barriers themselves, elect to participate in the service-learning project, noting their desire to be of assistance to their communities.

Three: Our students are the community.
The majority of our students are from our areas and are going to continue to live in them after their community college tenure. This is an important reality that can appeal to community partners looking to build long-term volunteers and may appeal significantly with civic engagement groups. Yet, as our neighboring universities are asked to serve as voting sites, receive visits from local and state candidates, and are included in voter engagement groups' target populations, our community college is often overlooked. Efforts to educate local boards of elections, local and state groups, and candidates by college administrators, boards, or civic engagement staff could result in increased political capital for our students.

Increased attention from external civic organizations, political candidates, or government agencies can lead to an increase in our students' commitment to civic participation, improve the college's or students' impact on local government decisions, and improve the likelihood that decision-making bodies recognize and value our students' voices, which is particularly important given that community college students often belong to groups traditionally underrepresented at the polls and/or in government positions. For example, during dialogues on political identity last fall, eager student participants commented that "no one ever talks to us about this stuff." We need to facilitate conversations that help students find their voice, and we need to ensure that key audiences are listening. For example, I recently took two students to a local board of elections meeting. The students were genuinely fascinated at seeing government in action and the board heard directly from our students that an early voting site on our campus matters to them.

Four: Our students' transformations through community engagement are long-lasting and deep.
Given our students limited financial resources, past life challenges, or even traumas, their community involvement can afford great personal gains when they are in a position to address the causes or lessen the effects of these hardships on others. Our students are not just acquiring awareness or augmenting classroom learning; they are experiencing personal transformation. For example, as part of her service-learning project, a student in my composition class who had survived domestic

abuse drafted a letter to her state representatives to advocate for better enforcement of a domestic violence victim notification law. During her in-class reflection, she teared up as she described how her children, who had witnessed her trauma, proudly placed the state legislator's response letter on their refrigerator in the same kitchen where she had been unexpectedly confronted by her former abuser when the state had failed to fulfill its notification law years prior. Being in the position to help solve the problem was transformational and powerful, not only for her, but for her children as well.

Five: Our students' transformative experiences don't require heavy lifting or perfectly-designed opportunities.

While we would love to offer our students weeklong immersive leadership training, international alternative break trips, or project-based interdisciplinary service-learning, our institutional budgets and students' life responsibilities make such community engagement largely infeasible. However, our students are still able to reap great benefit from experiences that require fewer resources and less commitment. For example, one of our campus food pantry shoppers, who also volunteers at our weekly pantry volunteer activity, feels supported by the service, but also valued for her contributions. This is an empowering shift for students who may be accustomed to being seen as a recipient rather than a provider or someone who can empower others.

Similarly, although we wrestled with having to forgo some depth in some service-learning projects, the outcomes for students were still life-changing. While we worried that settling for more student schedule-friendly, one-time events at multiple sites rather than a long-term service commitment to one community partner would limit impact, we did not find this to be true. For example, one of our first-generation students admitted that he chose to pursue a degree in computer programming because he felt he was "bad with people" and believed that working in this field would allow him to excel at something he liked while avoiding interpersonal interaction. His self-assessment, however, was challenged when he volunteered at a one-time event as part of a service-learning course and was assigned to be a greeter for a large community gathering. As he reflected in his service-learning portfolio, he was surprised at how much he had enjoyed those busy two hours and that he actually was very good at communicating and interacting with people. He had never seen himself in a leadership role, but through his engagement, he realized he had better people skills than he thought, and he admitted that he might consider a role as a team leader or manager someday.

This student likely would have been too intimidated to participate in a more advanced or collaborative community-based learning experience, and perhaps would not have gotten the chance to challenge his erroneous self-assessment. When faced with the choice of either blindly following best practices in community engagement or lowering barriers to our students' participation, we realized that what our students most need access to are the experiences themselves—even if they don't meet all the hallmarks of ideal service-learning—and this continues to guide our decision making. Scaled approaches to service-learning and community engagement allow us to meet students where they are.

Six: Our students' community engagement activities can have a significant effect on students' persistence.

Persistence and completion rates of community college students continue to garner national attention. Community engagement activities can be a part of the solution to the complex problem of student attrition by connecting students to the college, community resources, other students, or key staff. In fact, community engagement activities can fulfill all three factors that Vincent Tinto theorized were most critical to student persistence: self-efficacy, a sense of belonging, and relevance and value of the curriculum (Tinto, 2016).

One illustration of these related benefits at Durham Tech can be found in the story of a recent student who had been selected for a premier merit and need-based scholarship program that guaranteed admission to a prestigious university. He was also selected to serve as one of the college's voting fellows, whose role was to engage other students and lead voter registration, education, and mobilization activities. However, after the student's first semester, his GPA placed him on probation for the scholarship program. Although he registered for a full second semester of courses in the spring, he dropped them over the winter break due to financial challenges and a lack of family support. A conscientious and motivated student, he was eager to do well and realized that an opportunity was slipping through his fingers, but the reality of needing to work three jobs while also adjusting to college expectations was too great a challenge. Luckily, his fellowship work had provided him with a sense of pride and aligned with his personal goals of community organizing. He also had taken on a meaningful mentor role with one of the younger voting fellows. While he was technically not an enrolled student during the spring semester, he continued to meet biweekly with the staff member in charge of the voting fellowship. Through their conversations, he felt encouraged to take a late start spring course. The positive reinforcement from the fellowship kept him connected to the college and feeling he had something worthwhile to contribute and may enable him to keep on his academic journey with his guaranteed admission and scholarship.

Seven: Integrated initiatives serve the whole student.

At Durham Tech, service-learning students and co-curricular volunteers serve at area community partners, providing much-needed labor to our community but also learn about critical resources they or someone in their household may need. For example, students volunteering with Habitat for Humanity wondered how they, or close family members, could benefit from the program; another student volunteer who grew up in a Habitat House shared her family's experiences and the qualifications for the program. In another case, students who volunteered with an organization that addresses the achievement gap through literacy work left the experience with piles of books for their children. Finally, a service-learning student who assisted in a children's clothing closet later took her sister, who had recently given birth, to shop for free items because she was struggling to pay bills since having the baby.

Positive outcomes from overlapping experiences do not just happen off campus. One of the reasons our on-campus Harvest Food Pantry has been so successful and well-utilized can be traced to its co-location in our community engagement office, which students visit for a myriad of reasons. For some students, our office is a social space to come with their friends or classmates to get a snack. For others, it is where they get their family's weekly groceries or the gateway to other crisis supports on campus through our on-site social services benefits screening. Students also come to our space for ASB team meetings, cooking demonstrations with a nutritionist who provides free samples and recipes, or for club meetings.

The co-location not only means that students learn of helpful services while addressing another need. It also means that students and employees don't know who is coming and going: Is that student a pantry volunteer? A service-learning student dropping off release waivers? A homeless student needing toiletries? A student in one of our premier scholar programs trying to fulfill required volunteer hours? Someone working off court-ordered service hours? Or is that student seeking several of these things at once?

Our students lead complex lives with an interconnected web of influences and complications. Cross-trained, integrated, and/or co-located college departments provide a greater chance of assisting more of the students' needs effectively. Community engagement offices are uniquely positioned to lead this work.

Reflection and Next Steps

By reimagining what a community engagement office could look like, we were able to serve a true representation of our student population:

- The student who survived domestic abuse.
- The first-generation student who lacked opportunities to practice and assess his soft skills.
- The student living in public housing.
- The student experiencing homelessness.
- The student with financial struggles who lacks a safety net of family support.
- The student who doesn't see anyone representing her voice in public office.
- The student utilizing the food pantry who would otherwise skip meals to feed his children.

Although our original community engagement goals primarily focused on student learning and community impact, we've come to see our community engagement work as an imperative to ensure equity and inclusion and a way fulfill the democratization of higher education that community colleges were charged with decades ago. The students described above are students we have worked with through our office, but they also represent thousands of community college students across the country whose college educations are regularly interrupted by real life challenges, a fact that has been highlighted by the work of Sara Goldrick-Rab (2016) and recent studies from the Hope Center for College, Community, and Justice (Goldrick-Rab et al., 2019). Some think the barriers facing under-resourced students are too great for them to even be enrolled in college, much less for them to participate in curricular or co-curricular community engagement activities. But for many students, community involvement is exactly what they need.

Our community engagement programs are well-suited to support under-resourced students due to our familiarity with community resources and the connections we can make for students to these resources through volunteering and service-learning. We are also uniquely positioned to subvert the common stigma of utilizing a social service by blurring the lines between recipient and provider since our students who volunteer to help mitigate community needs may also be past or current beneficiaries of community programs. Engaging under-resourced populations can increase persistence, develop self-awareness, facilitate personal transformation, and make connections to the people and local organizations that will give students the confidence and tools to succeed in college and beyond.

Engaging with under-resourced students requires community engagement staff to question our policies and practices so that everyone is welcome and enabled to participate: Do we have a valid reason for every policy and practice, or are we simply copying other colleges' manuals and models? Are we regularly questioning what a student leader looks like, so we have a more inclusive definition that opens doors to life-changing opportunities? Do we offer transportation to all off-campus events or design events that students can bring their children to? Do we engage in service that reflects our student populations' lived experiences, such as events serving LGBTQ support centers, immigrant services, recovery houses, or homeless shelters?

Fulfilling the open-door policy of community colleges has not translated into overall student success partly because access alone does not constitute equity. We need to provide ways for under-resourced students to fully participate in higher education; it's not enough to let students into our colleges if we do not support them adequately once they are enrolled. Similarly, it is not enough to provide community engagement opportunities for students if only financially secure students can fully participate.

Conclusion

Revisioning community engagement in community colleges can create a structure that recognizes students struggling to meet basic needs, support those students through links to on- and off-campus resources, and empower students to feel they can overcome their problems and assist others. In other words, community engagement can be an essential piece of student success initiatives if we rethink and reframe our community engagement goals, including what practices we lift up as examples of quality engagement.

Community college community engagement should expand to recognize not only programs that meet widely regarded ideals, but also programs that are making a difference in students' lives in ways not typically measured with our assessments and evaluations. As colleges strive to acknowledge students' basic needs and follow lauded examples of wraparound services, community engagement should be part of the conversation. It is essential that we adapt our models by focusing on what works for our campus and our students and creatively adapt and apply benchmarks, rubrics, or commonly cited best practices. Opening up definitions and examples of quality service-learning, co-curricular service, and civic engagement provides space to elevate and celebrate activities that have not only lead to learning and awareness, but also student-centered support that meets our students where they are.

References

Goldrick-Rab, S. (2016). *Paying the price: College costs, financial aid, and the betrayal of the American Dream*. Chicago: The University of Chicago Press.

Goldrick-Rab, S., Baker-Smith, C., Coca, V., Looker, E. & Williams, T. (2019). College and university basic needs insecurity: A national #RealCollege report. Retrieved from https://hope4college.com/college-and-university-basic-needs-insecurity-a-national-realcollege-survey-report/

Kross, D. (2014, February 4). 7 reasons it's finally time to live in Research Triangle Park. Forbes Magazine. Retrieved from https://www.forbes.com/sites/davidkroll/2014/02/04/7-reasons-its-finally-time-to-live-in-research-triangle-park/#68f47806e1f9.

Ma, J. & Baum, S. (2016, April). Trends in community colleges: Enrollment, prices, student debt, and completion [PDF file]. College Board Research Briefs. Retrieved from https://trends.collegeboard.org/sites/default/files/trends-in-community-colleges-research-brief.pdf.

Tinto, V. (2016, September 26). From retention to persistence. Retrieved from https://www.insidehighered.com/views/2016/09/26/how-improve-student-persistence-and-completion-essay

Chapter 8

DEVELOPING AND ASSESSING HIGH-IMPACT, CLASSROOM-INTEGRATED SERVICE-LEARNING PROJECTS

Lori Moog
Emilie Stander

Raritan Valley Community College
Branchburg, New Jersey

This chapter discusses how the Raritan Valley Community College (RVCC) Service-learning Program engages students, faculty, administrators, and members of the community-at-large in service-learning in order to foster skills and values that contribute to the improvement of society, civic literacy, and students' career resiliency. Building on this mission, RVCC's Service-learning Program participated in a three-year, multistate grant project to assess students' service-learning outcomes. In a project funded by the Teagle Foundation, RVCC faculty and administrators worked with five other community colleges to implement pedagogical and curricular assessment in service-learning courses to evaluate the effectiveness of service-learning in preparing students to tackle big questions they experience and address important global issues through service-learning projects. In addition to assessment of student learning outcomes, RVCC uses a Student Engagement Transcript and the Carnegie Community Engagement Classification as tools for institutional benchmarking, self-assessment, and self-study. The benefits of such an approach will be discussed in the chapter.

The chapter also includes a description of how one RVCC faculty member designed and assessed a service-learning component in an introductory environmental science course, offering an evidence-based discussion of successes and lessons learned from that example. As a result of the Teagle project and other assessments, RVCC has reviewed and redesigned curricula, provided administrative support to faculty, and fostered an institutional culture committed to engagement in meaningful civic actions. Future plans include a comprehensive system of ongoing professional development on assessment to help faculty create stronger links between service-learning and curriculum development on numerous topics. It also will enable course-based community initiatives to be structured and coordinated across disciplines through cohort and peer approaches and thematically linked courses across semesters.

Background

Building on its mission and purpose, Raritan Valley Community College has cultivated a climate in which both the campus and its surrounding communities value learning and civic engagement. Concomitantly, the College offers programs and services that demonstrate its responsiveness to the community in addressing significant social concerns and believes that education can engage students as both learners and responsible citizens.

One of its hallmark programs is service-learning—a nationally recognized program that enables students to use community service as part of their coursework and receive credit for the experience. Each year, hundreds of students donate the economic equivalent of over $1,000,000 in service to more than 250 community organizations and their clients. From non-profits to schools to government agencies, students serve many different kinds of organizations that include pre-K-12 schools, English as a Second Language centers, after-school programs, nursing homes, adult day care centers, museums, libraries, court houses, probation departments, youth correctional facilities, environmental centers, farms, and homeless, domestic violence, and animal shelters. Students learn about important community issues while helping diverse populations that include minorities, low-income individuals, immigrants, at-risk children, families, single parents, and animals as well as the incarcerated, disabled, homeless, and elderly.

As part of an explicit effort to further develop student learning outcomes from service-learning experiences, Raritan Valley Community College's Service-learning program applied for and was awarded one of six community college service-learning grants from the New York-based Teagle Foundation during the Academic Years (AY) 2014 - 2016. The three-year grant enabled the six community colleges to work together to reflect on the larger aims of liberal arts education; develop replicable models that build students' current and future commitment to civic and moral responsibility; and assess students' learning outcomes from their service-learning projects. The Teagle Foundation extended the grant award to Raritan Valley Community College for dissemination of its best practices. The additional funding supported training workshops that were held at national conferences during AY 2017 and 2018.

In addition to Raritan Valley Community College, the other participating colleges in the three-year grant period included: Kingsborough Community College, Queensborough Community College, Mesa Community College, Kapi'olani Community College, and Delgado Community College. This work is relevant not only to community colleges but to all higher education institutions interested in developing students' civic and moral commitment to enhancing the quality of life in their communities.

Over the three-year grant period, the project involved faculty leads teaching the following courses:

- Foundations of Education, Grades 5 - 12
  Dr. Katherine Suk, Associate Professor of Elementary/Secondary Education
- Education Field Experience, Grades Preschool - 4
  Professor Kimberly Schirner, Associate Professor of Early Childhood Education
- Principles of Marketing and Business Administration
  Professor Tracy Rimple, Associate Professor of Business
- Introduction to Environmental Studies; Plants, Humans, and the Environment; Environmental Field Studies; Organic Agriculture
  Dr. Jay Kelly, Associate Professor of Biology
- Environmental Science & Sustainability
  Dr. Emilie Stander, Associate Professor of Environmental Science

- Trends in Nursing
  Professors Susan Williams and Heather Heithoff, Drs. Mary Balut and Beryl Stetson

All students enrolled in the above-mentioned classes were involved in various service-learning projects, with some examples following. Students enrolled in Environmental Field Studies were trained as citizen scientists. In partnership with the New Jersey Audubon Society, students in the course assessed forest conditions in central New Jersey and worked with local officials to improve forest health through science-based solutions.

Students enrolled in Plants, Humans, and the Environment and Organic Agriculture tapped invasive Norway maple (*Acer platanoides*) trees from early February through March at the 30-acre Forest Hill Preserve (FHP), a local town located near the college. The sap is collected to make maple syrup, teach students and citizens about maple syrup production, and raise funds for student conservation internships.

Students enrolled in Foundations of Education created "Teach2Matter at RVCC," a new initiative that offered pre-service teacher candidates a "mini-residency" by having them serve in local middle and high schools and engage other students in addressing important global issues.

Students enrolled in Trends in Nursing helped the South Branch Reformed Preschool with implementing a program whose initiative is to increase awareness of the importance of a healthy lifestyle through physical activity, and is based on Michelle Obama's "Let's Move" national campaign.

Project faculty were responsible for the following activities:

- Provide an orientation about the project for all students enrolled in the above-mentioned courses;
- Incorporate the "Big Question" as identified for the project in their course syllabus;
- Require all students to provide service to the community through either advocacy, direct or in-direct service, or a combination thereof;
- Have students submit reflection essays that address the "Big Question," as identified in the proposal;
- Collaborate with community partners to develop meaningful and appropriate placements for the project; oversee the above activities; guide reflections; participate in campus dialogs on the project; present at regional and/or national conferences; share their work within their department and with faculty in different departments to encourage

others to participate; and facilitate assessment;
- Verify the hours completed on their service-learning time sheet, which is used to create a Student Engagement Transcript to document students' out-of-classroom experiences. This official transcript documented students' participation in the Teagle project by course, placement, and hours, listing them as Teagle Scholars.

Student Engagement Transcript

The Student Engagement Transcript is an official college transcript that is an endorsement of service-learning and community service hours, leadership positions, civic engagement events attended, study abroad, internships, research projects, and more. The transcript is given to students alongside the traditional academic transcript, which students provide to prospective employers, transfer colleges, or graduate schools. The transcript helps students demonstrate how they achieved excellence in their chosen filed and learned the responsibilities of citizenship and service in the global community. This combination of academic and engagement transcripts provides a well-rounded representation of education, both inside and outside of the classroom, which enhances resumes, portfolios, and college applications. Students appreciate having the transcript to showcase all of their engagement work, and the feedback from employers and colleges has been extremely positive. It has helped students with their admission to colleges upon transfer and provided exemption from pre-requisites for certain programs of study. Employers also have used the transcript as part of the interview and hiring process.

The transcript is created in the College's main database, Banner. The information entered into the database is stored permanently and can be used for other assessments, such as a comparison of service-learning participants vs non-service-learning participants. The stored data can also be used to assess retention and graduation rates, time to degree completion, grade point average, demographics, etc.

The Teagle Foundation grant project offered a practical framework for helping students address significant social concerns, engaging them as learners and responsible citizens, and assessing their service-learning outcomes. The grant assessment project presented a set of well-tested strategies for assessing the impact of service-learning and civic engagement activities. Improvement and sustainability of service-learning experiences and partnerships were enhanced through formal assessment activities that involved the community, faculty, and students. The assessment process proved important for its role in communicating the value of service-learning to many different audiences. Learning how to document the impact of service-learning supported its institutionalization, facilitated its ability to translate community-based learning into scholarship, and fostered trust and communication among the various involved constituents.

Other assessment outcomes include the following:

- Helped faculty to document the impact of service-learning on student learning.
- Demonstrated the value of service-learning toward student learning.
- Used data-driven information for continuously improving the service-learning pedagogy.
- Demonstrated the rigor of this teaching method among colleagues.
- Helped faculty respond to students' questions of why they need to be involved in this type of learning.
- Taught students to consider the larger questions that lie outside boundaries of classroom work.
- Assisted faculty with improving the quality of student learning.
- Improved community partners' understanding about students' learning experience to help them better evaluate their work.
- Facilitated students' reflection on their service-learning experiences.
- Helped students recognize and view issues of social concern from multiple perspectives.
- Framed an informed opinion on community issues, learned from experiences.
- Related academic classroom work to practical applications on issues of social concern.
- Motived students to build capacity to take action in the community and in their personal lives.

Carnegie Classification

Since 2006, the Carnegie Foundation for the Advancement of Teaching has selected 392 colleges and universities for its elective classification on community engagement. The classification provides an established level of legitimacy, accountability, public recognition, and visibility. It can be a catalyst for efforts to improve teaching and learning through curricular connections to community-based problem solving as well as a tool for institutional benchmarking, self-assessment, and self-study.

Prior to the opening of the Classification, workshops are held nationally to learn what is needed to plan for the process, including forming a team, gathering data and information, and organizing and writing the application. The workshops help participants discover why and how to use the classification to benefit their service-learning and community engagement initiatives. The workshops also help participants consider how to improve their practice in assessment, reciprocal partnerships, faculty rewards, and integration and alignment with other institutional initiatives.

Carnegie Community Engagement Definition

Community engagement describes the collaboration between institutions of higher education and their larger communities (local, regional/state, national, global) for the mutually beneficial creation and exchange of knowledge and resources in a context of partnership and reciprocity. The purpose of community engagement is the partnership (of knowledge and resources) between colleges and universities and the public and private sectors to enrich scholarship and research and creative activity; enhance curriculum, teaching, and learning; prepare educated and engaged citizens; strengthen democratic values and civic responsibility; address critical societal issues; and contribute to the public good.

Institutional Assessment

In addition to assessing student performance, Raritan Valley Community College uses the Carnegie Community Engagement Classification to determine the effectiveness of the institution's community engagement work. The college received the 2008 Community Engagement Classification and the 2015 Reclassification.

Curricular example: Service-learning Teagle Foundation Project in Environmental Science and Sustainability, Dr. Emilie Stander

In my own first day of class as a college freshman in Introduction to Environmental Issues, the teaching assistants split us students into pairs and gave us bus schedules. Over the course of the semester, our role was to go into schools in Providence, RI, to teach environmental science to fourth-graders once each week. This was an eye-opening experience. Overnight I was forced to come out of the shell of my comfortable suburban background, navigate an urban public transportation system, interact with children from a wide diversity of backgrounds, and collaborate with professional educators to develop lesson plans and environment-oriented activities for youth. It was my first experience with service-learning, and I was immediately hooked. I found service-learning to be a means of connecting my academic learning to practicing the values and ethics that had drawn me to environmental issues as a teenager. It was an engine driving my academic and personal growth at the very beginning of my college experience. The service experiences I shared with my teaching partner and other students in the class formed the basis of friendships that persist to this day, over 20 years later.

Decades later, I found myself in a faculty position at Raritan Valley Community College (RVCC) in Branchburg, NJ, responsible for managing the environmental studies and science programs and teaching several environmental science courses. My personal experiences as an undergraduate, as well as my professional experiences as an educator, had convinced me to incorporate service-learning as an important part of the curriculum. As an educator in the environmental field, my overarching objective is to train the next generation of professionals to tackle our "wicked" environmental problems and thus make a positive contribution to society writ large and the communities where they will live and work. With its emphasis on civic engagement, service-learning was a natural fit for my courses and for my college's environmental studies and science programs.

RVCC's environmental science faculty aim to prepare students not only academically for environmental careers, but also by giving them real world experiences to assist them in developing critical technical skills, an ethic of civic engagement, and a means to contribute to meaningful solutions to environmental problems in their communities. I knew that service-learning as a pedagogical approach has numerous benefits, including the potential to increase student learning outcomes, success, and completion; provide opportunities to apply academic knowledge to real-world situations; and give students chances to build marketable technical and soft skills, explore career pathways, and interact with professionals in their future fields. Most importantly to me, I knew service-learning held the promise to help students see themselves as agents of change and build lifelong identities as civically responsible citizens involved in positive change on campus and in their local communities.

The only remaining questions for me were how best to design and implement service-learning in the environmental studies and science curricula and how to assess student learning outcomes from these experiences. I eased myself into implementation by plugging into my college's Service-learning program, directed by Lori Moog. Following initial conversations and coordination with Lori, I felt comfortable offering service-learning to students as an extra credit option in my introductory environmental issues and upper-level ecology courses. Lori had developed relationships with an impressive list of local environmental non-profit organizations that our students could approach for volunteer opportunities. Students participated in a minimum number of hours of service with these organizations, performing tasks such as trail maintenance, removal of invasive plants, and nature interpretation at local parks and wildlife refuges. To assess their learning outcomes, I required them to write an essay reflecting on their service activities and how these related to concepts we discussed in class.

Students who chose to participate in this mode of service-learning self-reported positive outcomes, including opportunities for professional development and networking, and an appreciation for civic engagement and associated personal satisfaction. However, from my perspective, I saw limitations in this mode of service-learning implementation. First, the quality of the reflection essays varied greatly. I had little to no involvement in the students' service experiences, and thus no role in guiding them toward an understanding of how their activities related to their academic experiences in the classroom. Because students were engaged in a wide variety of activities with different organizations, the essay prompts were quite general, which some students responded to beautifully, while others struggled to make the connections between academic concepts and their service activities. Also, students performed their service individually without opportunities to serve together, interact, and reflect with their peers, opportunities that in my own experience had been so critical to my personal growth as a college student. Finally, I felt that the organizations that accepted my students did not see their role as building the capacity of the next generation of environmental professionals; rather, my students were treated the same as all their other adult volunteers—as extra sets of hands for the tedious tasks that legitimately needed to get done. Overall, service-learning participation in my courses was low; over three semesters, 12 out of my 180 students, or seven percent, elected to perform service-learning. I felt this was a start, but represented only a partial achievement of my ambitious goals to foster an ethic of civic engagement in my courses.

During my third year of teaching, I had the opportunity to design a new introductory environmental science lab course that would be a requirement for environmental studies and science majors while also serving as a general education lab science course. At the same time, Lori invited me to participate in the Teagle Foundation service-learning grant program. I jumped at the opportunity to rethink my approach to the design and implementation of service-learning in my courses, and I was excited to try out the service-learning assessment tools that had been designed by other RVCC faculty and faculty from community colleges around the country. The "Big Question" developed by Bob Franco and his team at Kapi'olani inspired me to think bigger. I decided to "bake" service-learning directly into the framework of the course, such that a focused set of service-learning activities were integrated into the lab portion of the course; these activities were directly related to, and supported by, academic concepts covered during lecture. Early on in the course, we discussed water pollution, with a particular emphasis on non-point source pollution caused by stormwater runoff from impervious surfaces, like roads, roofs, and parking lots. Students completed a homework assignment in which they used publicly available databases and internet resources to find information about water quality in their local water bodies and in their drinking water. In sharing their results with their peers, they found many similarities among their towns and local communities and discovered that stormwater runoff is an important source of pollution to streams and rivers in the suburban watersheds my students live in. Engaging in solutions to this problem through our service-learning activities then became a way to enable students to apply their classroom learning to meaningful real-world situations where they live and work.

I reached out to two local environmental non-profit organizations that work on watershed protection and water quality issues, and was quickly connected to AmeriCorps volunteers embedded in both organizations who were eager to work with my students. The AmeriCorps volunteers delivered in-class and field-based trainings on stream assessment and rain garden maintenance techniques. Following these trainings, the students, under the collaborative supervision of the AmeriCorps volunteers and myself, assessed local streams and maintained rain gardens on and off campus. Both sets of actions have water quality implications; stream assessment results are shared with New Jersey's Department of Environmental Protection and are used to prioritize stream and watershed restoration efforts, and properly maintained rain gardens absorb stormwater from roads and roofs and filter out many pollutants through soil and plant functions while allowing the water to slowly drain to groundwater. Students completed 20 hours of service, documented their work, and presented their findings through both written group reports and poster presentations on campus. They also wrote individual reflective essays utilizing the standardized Teagle essay prompts.

One of my goals in designing the service-learning component of the course this way was to address several of the course learning objectives. In particular, I expected that through their service-learning activities, students would be able to:

1. Understand ethical issues and situations related to environmental issues,
2. Apply the scientific method to analyze environmental problems and draw conclusions from data and evidence.
3. Prepare written reports and/or poster presentations of environmental and sustainability research/practice in a technical format.

Another major goal of mine was to design service-learning to address my students' emotional needs. After several semesters teaching the non-lab version of the introductory environmental issues course, I had identified a problem with the course design. A large amount of the course content focused on identifying and describing environmental issues, such as water pollution, toxic chemicals in consumer products, and air pollution, all of which have public and environmental health implications. We discussed the roles of government agencies, private companies, and consumer choices in contributing to these problems. Initially, as their awareness increased, students enjoyed exploring the nuances and complexities of environmental problems and their institutional and collective sources, but as the course wore on, I began to see an emotional shift emerge among a portion of the students. As the enormity and complexity of the problems become clearer, students begin experiencing and expressing negative emotions, including fear and hopelessness. Despite the fact that we discussed solutions to all these problems, many doubted the will of individuals and public and private institutions to make the changes necessary to adequately address our environmental challenges. This is particularly pronounced around the issue of climate change, which they correctly recognize has the potential to very negatively impact their future quality of life.

I began to see service-learning as an antidote to these negative emotions; service-learning allowed students to channel their anger and fear beyond simply defining and describing environmental problems to personally and collectively engaging in solutions in their local communities. Not only could students understand their own individual contributions to positive change through their activities, but they also collaborated with other students and with professionals from organizations whose missions include making positive change on a larger, collective scale.

Anecdotal results indicate that many intended and unintended benefits were achieved through the service-learning experience. I was able to witness the professional and personal growth of many students through their informal interactions with peers, AmeriCorps volunteers, and myself. Students were trained by other young people (i.e., the AmeriCorps volunteers) just a few years older than themselves in technical skills that are in demand in the environmental field. Students had the opportunity to ask the volunteers about their college experiences at four-year institutions as well as their professional experiences at environmental non-profit organizations soon after they obtained their bachelor's degrees. For their part, AmeriCorps volunteers benefited because they were able to earn credit toward their AmeriCorps requirements for the trainings they delivered and for the time they spent supervising students in the field. The partnership between RVCC and the two environmental organizations has led to additional collaborative projects among these institutions that will likely allow additional service-learning and co-curricular activities to emerge in the future.

The rubric scores from the Teagle essays indicate that the academic and personal growth objectives were achieved to an encouraging degree. Students were able to articulate the water quality problems on campus and in the local community and describe how their service-learning activities contributed to solutions to those problems. Over three semesters, students scored an average of 2.6 out of 4 in the relevant rubric criteria. Students were also able to explain how their service-learning activities related to concepts covered during lecture (average rubric score of 2.7 out of 4 over three semesters). Some remarked that their understanding of key course concepts improved because they could see how the concepts are applied in the real world. Many students indicated that the service-learning experiences influenced their course selection and/or choice of major and career path (average rubric score of 2.5 out of 4 over three semesters). Many also reported changing their personal habits and behaviors related to the environment and expressed a desire to influence the behaviors of friends and family to better protect the environment (average rubric score of 2.4 out of 4 over three semesters). A number of students indicated a desire to join the campus Environmental Club and/or volunteer for local environmental organizations.

The rubric scores also pointed to areas for improvement. Students did not perform as successfully on the assessment criteria related to civic and moral engagement. For example, the average rubric scores of 1.9 out of 4 during the first two semesters in explaining water quality as a public issue and 1.8 out of 4 in identifying issues of unfairness or injustice related to water quality indicated that while students were comfortable describing their own experiences related to water quality, they were less comfortable imagining the experiences of other members of our communities. This came as a surprise, since we discuss environmental justice during lecture related to the Flint water crisis and e-waste recycling in the developing world. I hypothesized that students needed to see environmental justice examples related to water quality closer to home, and made some adjustments to the service-learning and lecture curriculum to address this need, including inviting an environmental professional to give a guest lecture on environmental justice projects related to brownfield redevelopment along the Delaware River in Camden, NJ. As a result of these modifications, average rubric scores improved to 2.4 and 2.8 out of 4 on the aforementioned civic and moral engagement criteria during the Fall 2016 semester.

Now that the Teagle Foundation grant is completed, I have begun the process of adjusting the language in the reflection essay prompts and rubric to better match my specific course activities and learning objectives. I continue to modify the lecture portion of the course to explore environmental justice issues, particularly related to water quality, early and often during the semester, and I make a point of using local examples where possible. Students are required to reflect on these issues through several homework assignments during the lecture portion of the class, so that by the time they tackle the service-learning essay, they are more accustomed to articulating in writing their thoughts and feelings related to environmental justice. Finally, I plan to assess the course in the near future, and will integrate an assessment of how well the service-learning activities facilitated student mastery of the three relevant course learning objectives.

The service-learning activities continue to be a rewarding experience for many of the students. In their reflective essays they often report on the benefits they feel they have received. Here, in their own words, are some examples of self-reported benefits, in terms of:

1. Personal growth:
   "I feel much more confident pursuing job/career opportunities thanks to real life knowledge I gained from the course and service-learning. It helped me understand the different types of careers and the reality of the type of work involved in environmental sciences."
2. Applying academic knowledge to real world situations:
   "The service-learning opportunities made me realize I work better and harder when I spend time outside and get hands-on with the information I study in class, and that helped me pick my transfer school."
3. Viewing themselves as agents of change:
   "I can now consider myself an agent of change because of the work I've done in my service-learning activities, the personal changes I've made in my life thanks to the knowledge I have gained from the coursework, and through the knowledge I can now spread to promote change in my family and friends' lives."

Looking Forward

The Teagle Foundation Assessment project fostered greater faculty collaboration on how to develop service-learning courses and assessment practices while also strengthening community partnerships. As a result, the Faculty Leads in the project now serve as mentors to other faculty members on campus and at other colleges and universities.

Because community involvement and partnership are important to RVCC, the models developed and lessons learned from this grant are being disseminated to the community-at-large. Many opportunities exist to promote and continue the work of this project. The Service-learning program maintains an office dedicated to working with full-time and part-time faculty within all academic departments. As part of the orientation and training, assistance is given to help faculty incorporate the service-learning pedagogy and assessment into different courses. Additionally, the Service-learning program organizes campus-community events that include conferences, faculty development workshops, and forum discussions on special topics. These events enable RVCC to serve as a model for other community colleges, as well as schools from the kindergarten-through-high school levels, helping these institutions to develop similar programs and practices.

It is anticipated that, because of this project, the service-learning curriculum at RVCC will move forward by instilling a high level of understanding and advocacy for service-learning and assessment initiatives both on campus and in the community. Intended outcomes are to develop model strategies that integrate information and current practices about the topic into many different courses, promote partnerships between schools and the community that will help sustain the effort, and encourage the development of good citizenship practices. The process of involving students, faculty, and community members over the three-year project period helped to establish an important awareness on campus and in the community about service-learning and assessment, while also encouraging greater participation in civic activities.

Chapter 9

PUBLIC ACHIEVEMENT

Increasing Student Persistence and Completion through Robust Political Experiences

John J. Theis
Lone Star College- Kingwood
Kingwood, TX

Colleges and universities have always had a major role in developing the civic capacities of our young people. However, we have lost our focus on this role. As we have lost that focus, our persistence and graduation rates have declined. Overall, college completion rates are at abysmally low levels. The declines are across the board, but community college rates are especially poor (Fain, 2015). Fewer than 40% of community college students earn a degree or certificate within 6 years of enrollment (Bailey et. al., 2015). This is particularly problematic since community colleges are the institution of higher education that serves the largest share of low income and minority students.

In the fall of 2015, community colleges served 41% of all US undergraduates. Due to the cost of higher education, 44% of low-income students (those with family incomes below $25,000 per year) attend community colleges as their first college out of high school. In addition, 56% of Native Americans, 52% of Hispanics, 42% of African Americans, and 39% of Asian/Pacific Islanded attend community college (AACC, 2017). Put simply, community colleges are a pathway to upward mobility for the poor and minority populations of the United States. This makes the low graduation rates even more troublesome, as attending community college as a way up becomes, for many, another burden with costs and time commitments that do not lead to any tangible benefits. Due to the "graduation problem," the Texas Legislature in 2013 tied its funding of community colleges to retention and completion in an attempt to force community colleges to deal with the problem.

This chapter argues that one way to increase student persistence and graduation is to offer students robust political experiences that tie academic content to real-world issues and help students develop a sense of agency and an ability to navigate complex systems. This chapter provides an example of a participatory program, Public Achievement, which has proven to not only increase graduation rates of students at a community college but develop civic skills, capacities, and agency as well.

Barriers to Community College Completion

Studies have identified two main barriers to community college completion. Bailey characterizes the structure of community colleges as "cafeteria" style. As Levesque (2018, section 2, paragraph 2) notes, "completing a credential or degree requires students to sort through an overwhelming amount of information to make complicated decisions, such as what to major in, what courses to take to satisfy program requirements, whether and how to get involved in a job training program, whether and how to transfer to a four-year program, and what kind of job to pursue after graduation." Students become overwhelmed in an environment that seems foreign to them. Often there are insufficient advisors to help students navigate the maze of choices, and students are often allowed to simply enroll online without ever meeting with an advisor.

A second set of issues is the motivational barriers to completion. One key motivational barrier is the perceived disconnect between a student's coursework and its connection to their lives (Karp, 2011). As Karp notes, "Students who do not see the value of their coursework often behave in counterproductive ways, by failing to complete coursework or dropping required courses" (p. 12).

Community colleges are seeking to address these issues by creating a variety of new programs and processes within the college. Programs such as "First-Year Experience," or mandatory advising of first-year students and "Guided Pathways" have been set up to address these issues, with some success (Scrivner et al., 2015). While providing more supports and simplifying complex processes may be helpful, these programs also may be dealing with the symptoms of the problem rather than dealing with the problem itself. There has been a tendency to streamline degree plans, weeding out classes that may not be "essential to the major." In Texas, the requirements for an associate's degree have been dropped to 60 hours, leading to debates and disagreements as to whether a second English class or speech class should be removed from the core.

As a professor of government, I am acutely aware of students' views that my class is not related to their career. On the first day of class, I always ask my students whether they are excited to take a government class. The blank stares and frowns say it all. When I ask them why they are in the class, 9 out of 10 say, "because it is a requirement." I have no illusion that most students see no connection between a government class and their career when they enter my classes, so I work very hard to make sure that by the time they take their final they see it as important.

While simplifying the complex systems of college may improve persistence and graduation, it does little to help students learn to navigate complex systems of life: whether that be in their career, their families, or communities. Some of the key skills a college degree provides are the tools to be successful in a variety of environments and systems (and virtually none of them will be changed to help graduates be more successful). It is more important to teach students to learn to navigate complex systems and, in some ways, this is what higher education is really about. Employers have repeatedly testified that twenty-first-century employees need training in a broad general education such as history, global cultures, intercultural literacy, ethical judgment, and civic engagement. Technical skills are important, but employers underscore that for today's economy, technical skills are not enough (A Crucible Moment, 2012; Hart Research Associates, 2010; Peter D. Hart Research Associates 2006, 2008).

Developing Civic Capacities in Community College Students

Today, people are questioning the value of broad-based liberal arts training in history, philosophy, and literature as our society moves increasingly toward a technocratic culture. Community colleges have followed suit, emphasizing job training and workforce development over the broad-based learning demanded for more educated citizens. Yet, I would argue that the broad-based learning that gave rise to public higher education is valuable precisely because it teaches skills that help young people learn to navigate the world. We have forgotten John

Adams's advice to his son: "You will ever remember that all the end of study is to make you a good man and a useful citizen." When the Constitution's framers talked about education, they did not just mean vocational training or apprenticeships. "While this type of training was certainly important, they also wanted a citizenry trained in government, ethics (moral philosophy), history, rhetoric, science (natural philosophy), mathematics, logic, and classical languages, for these subjects made people informed and civil participants in a democratic society" (Fea, 2012, paragraph 9). It is precisely these skills that make people "informed and civil participants" that help people work within complex systems. Even as community colleges move toward more focused job-oriented education, the business community is reemphasizing the importance of the broad-based skills that formed the basis of higher education in a previous era.

Early educational reformers reflected this relationship between education and citizenship. Horace Mann, an early advocate for public education and the father of "Common Schools" explicitly contended that democracy requires educated citizens. John Dewey, a leading reformer of public education at the turn of the century said: "Democracy cannot flourish where the chief influences in selecting subject matter of instruction are utilitarian ends narrowly conceived for the masses, and, for the higher education of the few, the traditions of a specialized cultivated class…" (Dewey, 1966). These authors seem more prescient than many would give them credit for.

By beginning to incorporate a broader definition of the importance and utility of a college degree, at an earlier stage of a student's college experience and throughout its duration, students would find their college experiences more meaningful and more compelling. Those students would also be more likely to internalize those experiences and end up being more persistent. These are two interrelated reasons that help account for the fundamental transformative nature of traditional college degrees and help to explain why people with higher levels of education have increased levels of political participation and an increased ability to survive the vicissitudes of the economy and society in an increasingly complex world. If the only reason a student decides to attend college is to get a job and the only benefits they get from a college education are narrow utilitarian job skills, then the student will be more likely to drop out and quit when a job comes along. That student is then likely to find themselves right back in the position that brought them to college in the first place, a year or five down the road, as the vagaries of the market lead to layoffs, bankruptcies, and unemployment.

Historically, colleges and universities have always had a major role in developing the capacities of our citizens. Civic skills have a documented and important relationship to college success. Many studies have documented the role civic engagement and service play in improving student performance rates (Astin & Sax, 1998; Brownell & Swaner, 2010; Gallini & Moely 2003; Nigro & Farnsworth, 2009; Vogelgesang et al., 2002). As one study concluded, "College students who participate in civic engagement learning activities not only earn higher grade point averages but also have higher retention rates and are more likely to complete their college degree" (Cress et al. 2010, p. 1). Despite the increasing pressures for and emphasis on success, most college success programs have ignored this important connection. Civic engagement develops agency in students, and students who feel they have more control and influence over their environment are more likely to succeed. In the areas of engaged citizenship, there is only ad hoc instructor-driven emphasis and little systematic institution-wide exploration of these areas as a priority. However, all college courses can and should play a role in helping students to develop agency.

Finally, former Lockheed Martin CEO Norman Augustine (2011) has pointed out that "students' weak grasp of history actually threatens America's economy as well as its freedom. Narrow training is bad preparation for the economy as well as for democracy" (quoted in A Crucible Moment, 2012). At a time when issues facing society are becoming more complex, broad-based education with more intense critical thinking skills aimed at building collaborative capacities in students are more, not less, important.

In the end, students who see themselves as agents in their own future should have higher levels of retention and completion. Students who have developed a sense of empowerment will feel more capacity to overcome obstacles and move toward completing their degrees. Students with a sense of empowerment will be better able to move through the complex systems that will face them for the rest of their lives.

Challenges to Civic Education

Civic Education in most of America's colleges and universities has essentially taken one of three paths. It has been relegated to political science classes where one learns about institutions, parties, and voting. The second avenue for civic education at most American colleges is student life and the amalgamation of student clubs and extra-curricular activities that focus on citizenship and leadership. These are most often seen in the College Democrat or Republican clubs, debate teams, Get Out the Vote drives and student government. The final area of civic learning in higher education is volunteerism and service-learning (Carcasson, 2013). Very few civic activities in higher education see students as co-creators of their civic life, but rather, they emphasize a passive or subordinate view of students in their communities.

The challenge for any institution of higher learning is to get beyond contemporary forms of political education in colleges, whether that be a lecture-based government class, joining the college democrats or volunteerism to tie rich civic experiences to concepts and skills from a student's coursework across the curriculum. As Ronan (2011) points out, civic engagement must move the whole person along a continuum from Civics, Voting, and Patriotism towards Deliberation, Concord, and Public Action. Deliberation, Concord, and Public Action are crucial to civic engagement because they provide students with the skills to tackle the problems of democracy. Civic engagement strategies that emphasize students as actors in the system and seek to build empowerment skills become the essential mechanism to move from patriotism, voting, and civics toward deliberation, concord, and public action. Moving along that spectrum is essential for solving the problems of democracy and can impact student success. The civic skills Ronan identifies are not knowledge and data-based but rather, experience-based.

Ultimately, for real education to occur, we must move toward a more holistic notion of education that seamlessly incorporates skills that empower students and provide them with critical thinking and problem-solving experiences across the scope of campus life, from the classroom to the dorms. This is the only way that students will learn to be powerful actors in their communities (wherever that may be) and learn to work through the problems that can occur in the systems we all find ourselves embedded in.

Public Achievement at Lone Star College-Kingwood

At Lone Star College-Kingwood, where I currently teach, the Center for Civic Engagement has begun to develop programs to teach students democratic skills. A centerpiece has been the development of Public Achievement. Public Achievement is a youth engagement initiative developed at the Center for Democracy and Citizenship at Augsburg

College in Minneapolis, Minnesota. In the Public Achievement model, college and K-12 students' partner in teams to research and develop action plans to address issues in their community.

Since the program started at LSC-Kingwood, over 200 students have worked with students in two area high schools, one elementary school, and one special education program. LSC-Kingwood students currently work with Cleveland ISD's Southside Primary school and Humble ISD special needs students in the Northeastern suburbs of Houston, Texas. Last year there were 57 college students and over 80 elementary and 18 special education students working in 13 issue groups. Participating students choose issues and form action groups around those issues. College students serve as coaches for the action groups as they research the issue, develop action plans, and carry out those plans. The issues range from parochial ones, such as improving school lunches or school playgrounds and addressing bullying, to larger community-wide issues, such as building a community teen center and stopping animal abuse or impacting homelessness. Regardless of the issue, college coaches and action team participants must learn to access power by discovering who has it and what their interests are. They must learn to articulate their self-interest, ask questions, craft appeals, listen to feedback, and modify proposals based on stakeholder interests. In Public Achievement, participants need to adapt to be successful; they cannot count on pushing their proposals through. Instead they must find ways to shape their ideas to satisfy multiple and often competing stakeholders and providing each with some level of investment in a shared outcome. These are crucial civic skills, but they are also the same skills students need to navigate the college environment.

Public Achievement at LSC-Kingwood began in 2010 using volunteer coaches from Phi Theta Kappa, the community college honors society, where the program served as their "Honors in Action" project. During the 2011-2012 school year, students volunteered to be coaches and then during the 2012-13 school year, the coaches were students enrolled in an Introduction to Political Science class. In the fall of 2013, a change in the state-mandated curriculum from a two-course sequence in US and Texas politics to a dedicated US Politics class and a dedicated Texas Politics class provided an opportunity to integrate Public Achievement into the college core. Public Achievement was incorporated into a section of the Texas Politics course. For 4 years, the Public Achievement program resided in Govt. 2306, section 2001, a Texas politics class taught on Monday and Wednesday mornings. The data in this paper reflect students enrolled in Introduction to Political Science in 2012-2013 and Texas Politics in the remaining years. Public Achievement took a brief hiatus from the classroom in the 2017-2018 school year as Hurricane Harvey flooded the Kingwood Campus and virtually all classes were moved online. I recruited 2 volunteers to work with me and we continued coaching students at 2 sites. During the 2018-2019 school year, as our campus reopened, Public Achievement moved back into the classroom, but the data from that year is not available at the time of this writing.

Table 9.1 Public Achievement Student Retention and Completion by Year

	2012-2013	2013-2014	2014-2015	2015-2016	2016-2017	Total
Participants (total)	11	28	39	54	54	186
Fall	7	7	19	29	27	89
Spring	4	21	20	25	27	97
Earned Degree	10 (90.1)	18 (64.3)	23 (59)	26 (48.1)	31 (57.4)	108 (58.1)
LSC-K	17.3	11.8	13.0	19.4	17.2	
Fall-to-Spring Persistence	7 (100)	5 (71)	17 (89)	21 (72)	21 (78)	71 (79.8)
LSC-K	69.5	70.4	69.4	71.9	71.4	
Fall-to-Fall Persistence	6 (54.5)	16 (57.1)	22 (56.4)	35 (64.8)	34 (63)	113 (60.8)
LSC-K	47.1	47.4	47.1	46.4	46.6	

The above table reflects the breakdown of student outcomes. What becomes immediately clear from the data are the high persistence rates for students involved in Public Achievement. The table shows the course enrollments for the year and breaks them down by fall and spring semesters. Persistence is looked at by examining the fall-to-spring persistence for students in the fall sections and fall-over-fall persistence for all students. LSC-Kingwood's general student population (LSC-K) is examined in the table as well.

What becomes very clear in looking at the results of these programs is that participants have good persistence and graduation rates. Students in Public Achievement had a 58% graduation rate over the five years. This is more than three times the graduation rate of LSC-K students of the same 5-year period. In addition, it is almost as high as the 6-year graduation rate of 4-year colleges which currently stands at 60%. In addition, the fall to spring as well as the fall to fall persistence rates are significantly higher than the campus as a whole.

What might explain the results? During the 2012-2013 year when students were enrolled in the Introduction to Political Science classes, most of the students had a relationship with me, as they had been enrolled in one of my other classes. I recruited students to make sure there was sufficient enrollment. However, when the PA program was moved into the Texas Politics class, students chose to sign up and most of the students did not know me. These students took the class because it was required. Students involved in Public Achievement learn how to navigate a complex community. They have to learn to ask questions to discover how to accomplish goals; they must research problems they want to work on; they must figure out who has power and build alliances with other actors. They have to learn to be citizens in a democracy, and in doing so they see how a government class matters in the real world.

Conclusion

As previously stated, colleges and universities have always had a major role in developing the civic capacities of our young people, but as we have lost that focus, our persistence and graduation rates have declined. One way to increase student persistence and graduation is to offer robust political experiences like Public Achievement that serve to tie academic content to real-world issues and help students develop a sense of agency and an ability to navigate complex systems. Rather than simplifying the college experience, the key is to help them acquire the skills to navigate complex systems. Civic skills allow students to do that. We would hope students would be clearer on how government functions after taking a government class. However, a government class where Public Achievement is an integral component not only teaches the formal structures, but the students also get hands-on experience in the vast, unseen underbelly of the political system and gain experience navigating it.

References

American Association of Community Colleges. (2017). Fast facts. Retrieved from https://www.aacc.nche.edu/research-trends/fast-facts/

Astin, A. W. & Linda J. S. (1998). How undergraduates are affected by service participation. *Journal of College Student Development, 39*(3), 251–63.

Augustine, N. (2011, September 21). The education our economy needs." *Wall Street Journal*. Retrieved from https://www.wsj.com/articles/SB10001424053111904265504576568351324914730

Bailey, M. J., & Dynarski, S. M. (2011). Inequality in postsecondary education. Duncan, G. & Murnane, R., (Eds.), *Whither opportunity?: Rising inequality, schools, and children's life chances* (pp. 117-131). New York: Russell Sage Foundation.

Brownell, J. E. & Swaner, L. E. (2010). *Five high-impact practices: Research on learning outcomes, completion, and quality*. Washington, DC: Association of American Colleges and Universities.

Carcasson. M. (2013). *Rethinking civic engagement on campus: The overarching potential of deliberative practice*. Dayton, OH: Kettering Foundation.

Cress, C. M., Burack, C., Giles Jr., D. E., Elkins, J., & Stevens, M.C. (2010). *A promising connection: Increasing college access and success through civic engagement*. Boston: Campus Compact.

Dewey, J. (1966). *Democracy and education: An introduction to the philosophy of education*. New York: Free Press.

Fain, P. (2015, November 17). College completion rates decline more rapidly. *Inside Higher Education*. Retrieved from https://www.insidehighered.com/quicktakes/2015/11/17/college-completion-rates-decline-more-rapidly

Fea, J. (2012). Education for a democracy. *Patheos*. Retrieved from https://www.patheos.com/resources/additional-resources/2012/03/education-for-a-demoracy-john-fea-03-14-2012.aspx.

Gallini, S. M. & Moely, B. E. (2003). Service-learning and engagement, academic challenge, and retention. *Michigan Journal of Community Service-learning, 10*(1), 5–14.

Hart Research Associates. (2010). *Raising the bar: Employers' views on college learning in the wake of the economic downturn*. Washington, DC: Association of American Colleges and Universities.

Karp, M, M. (2011). *Toward a new understanding of non-academic student support: Four mechanisms encouraging positive student outcomes in the community colleges*. Community College Research Center. New York, NY: Teachers College, Columbia University.

Levesque, E. M. (2018). Improving community college completion rates by addressing structural and motivational barriers. Washington DC: Brookings Institute. Retrieved from https://www.brookings.edu/research/community-college-completion-rates-structural-and-motivational-barriers/.

Nigro, G. & Farnsworth, N. (2009). *The effects of service-learning on retention: A report to the Northern New England Campus Compact.* Boston, MA: Campus Compact.

Peter D. Hart Research Associates. (2006). *How should colleges prepare students to succeed in today's global economy?* Washington, DC: Association of American Colleges and Universities.

Peter D. Hart Research Associates. (2008). *How should colleges assess and improve student learning?: Employers' views on the accountability challenge.* Washington, DC: Association of American Colleges and Universities.

Ronan, B. (2011). *The civic spectrum: How students become engaged citizens.* Dayton, Ohio: Kettering Foundation.

Scrivener, S., Weiss, M. J., Ratledge, A., Rudd, T., Sommo, C., & Fresques, H. (2015). "Doubling graduation rates: Three-year effects of CUNY's Accelerated Study in Associate Programs (ASAP) for developmental education students." New York, NY: MDRC.

The National Task Force on Civic Learning and Democratic Engagement. (2012). *A crucible moment: College learning and democracy's future.* Washington, DC: Association of American Colleges and Universities.

Vogelgesang, L. J., Ikeda, E. K., Gilmartin, S. K., & Keup, J. R. (2002). Service-learning and the first-year experience: Learning from the research.

Zlotkowski, E. A. (Ed.), *Service-learning and the first-year experience: Preparing students for personal success and civic responsibility* (pp. 15–26). National Center for The First-Year Experience and Students in Transition. Columbia, SC: University of South Carolina.

Chapter 10

THE ARC OF ASSESSMENT LEADS TO STUDENT SUCCESS AND SOCIAL AND ENVIRONMENTAL JUSTICE

Kapiʻolani's Service and Sustainability Learning Program

Robert Franco
Krista Hiser
Francisco Acoba

Kapi'olani Community College
Honolulu, Hawaii

In this chapter, we highlight important moments in the development of Kapiʻolani Community College's service-learning assessment practices over the last 10 years. We start with the College's history and innovation with regard to high impact practices. Then, we describe the College's assessment framework, the Kapiʻolani Engagement, Learning, and Achievement Model, or KELA. We detail one aspect of that framework—Learning—as represented by the end-of-semester reflection essay, which is aligned with the college's general education student learning outcomes. Finally, we discuss our assessment of sustainability courses. The modifications we have made to our assessment model over time suggest that service-learning is always necessarily changing. Since our efforts are focused on transforming institutional and community concerns, our curricula and assessments to address them must necessarily transform as well.

Kapi'olani Community College: Campus Profile

In 2019, Kapi'olani Community College, located on the slopes of Diamond Head in Honolulu on the island of O'ahu, was the largest two-year campus in the ten college University of Hawai'i (UH) system. The College enrollment in spring 2019 was 6,187 students, with an average age of 24.7. The College is designated as a Native Hawaiian-serving institution by the U.S. Department of Education and serves a richly multicultural student population. Students' ancestries connect Hawai'i with the region, nation, and world: one in six students is Native Hawaiian, one in eight is Caucasian, one in two is Asian, and one in six is mixed race (two or more races). The mix of Pacific Islanders, African American, Hispanic and American Indian students, along with 800 international students, contribute to a uniquely indigenous, intercultural and international learning environment. Nearly sixty percent of students is female, and two in three students are part-time. The College conferred more than 1,300 degrees and certificates annually from fiscal year 2014-2015 through 2017-2018 and transferred more than 600 students to four-year universities in 2014-2015 and 2015-2016.

Commitment to Innovation and High Impact Practices

Throughout the 1990s and into the 2000s, the College was committed to an Asia-Pacific Emphasis and an International and Global Education Emphasis that were nationally recognized by the Association for American Colleges and Universities (AAC&U) and the American Council on Education (ACE). In 1995, the College initiated its Service-Learning Emphasis wherein student could serve and learn in Honolulu's multicultural communities and public schools. Each of these Emphases were formally endorsed by the College's Faculty Senate. In 2000, the College was selected as a "Greater Expectations" institution for its Asia-Pacific and Service-Learning Emphases. About the same time, it engaged in ACE's "Lessons Learned in Assessing Global Learning Program" and developed learning assessment methods, practices, and protocols focused on student development of "global competence."

From 1995 to 2013, the College was strongly supported by Hawaii-Pacific Islands Campus Compact and the Corporation for National Service as it deepened and developed faculty understanding and practice of service-learning and community and civic engagement. The focus on faculty development was also strongly supported by the Community College Center for Community Engagement (formerly the Campus Compact Center for Community Colleges) and their annual summer conferences. In 2006, the College was deeply engaged in the development of the Carnegie Foundation's Elective Classification for Community Engagement, which required greater attention to strong institutional engagement and support for student and faculty engagement in community development. The College remains committed to Service-Learning and Diversity/Global Learning with a sharpened focus on Native Hawaiian language, culture and history, as well as Writing Intensive Courses and a First-Year Experience program.

Kapiʻolani Engagement, Learning and Achievement (KELA) Model

From 2006 to the present, increased emphasis on student assessment and student success by the Accrediting Commission for Community and Junior Colleges (ACCJC) of the Western Association of Schools and Colleges (WASC), drove the continuous improvement of the Kapiʻolani Engagement, Learning and Achievement institutional assessment model. The College has developed the model as a means to evaluate progress toward Strategic Plan goals as well as the effects of specific innovations or "treatments," such as service-learning and sustainability, on student engagement, learning, and achievement.

In 2018, a comprehensive accreditation review by the Accreditation Commission for Community and Junior Colleges (ACCJC) of the Western Association of Schools and Colleges (WASC), commended the College "for its design of the Kapiʻolani Engagement, Learning, and Achievement (KELA) model [as] an exemplary structure that incorporates student engagement throughout the system of institutional effectiveness measures." (ACCJC Report 2019).

The campus strategic plans from 2009-2015 were strongly aligned with this assessment framework. In the original KELA version, the "solar energy" in the center was "High Impact Practices" rather than "Student Success Pathway." This energy was to drive further faculty development of teaching practices to help the College reach its stated engagement, learning and achievement goals.

Figure 11.1: Kapi'olani Engagement, Learning, and Achievement Model

Engagement measures are derived from the Community College Survey of Student Engagement (CCSSE), while Achievement Measures are derived from the UH System Program Reviews and Strategic Planning. Learning assessments were focused on course and general education outcomes, and the Service-Learning Emphasis led the College's assessment of general education.

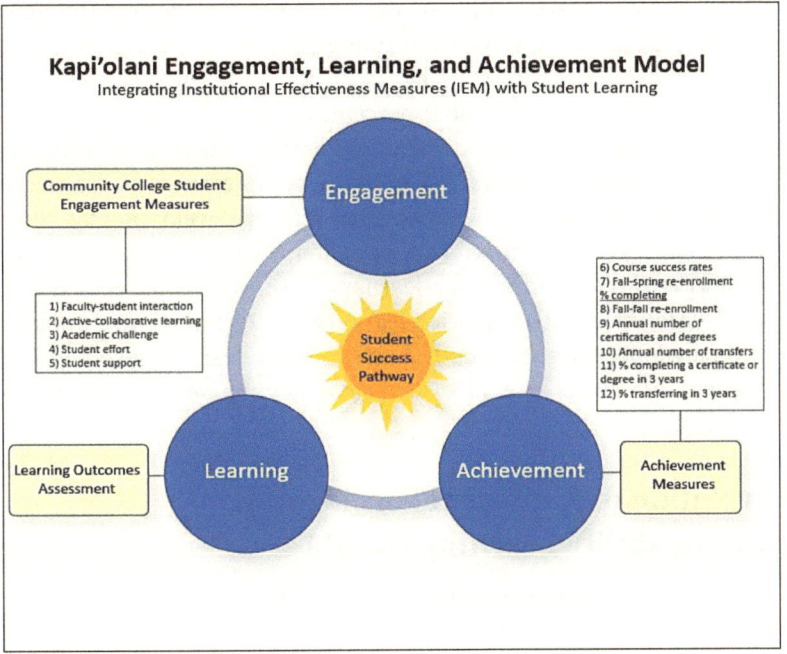

Service-Learning and the KELA Model

To examine the relevance and usefulness of the KELA model in assessing specific innovations and their impact on student success (engagement + learning + achievement), institutional researchers and service-learning lead faculty focused on service-learning as a specific academically based "treatment."

In 2014, we were able to demonstrate that service-learning, as a research-based high impact practice, resulted in higher levels of engagement as measured by student scores on the CCSSE (Yao Hill et al. 2014).

In short, our study showed that service-learning was a positive academic treatment in terms of Engagement and Achievement, two of the three measures on the College's institutional effectiveness framework. After controlling for students' demographics and academic background, service-learners scored 10.7 percent higher on active-collaborative learning, 5.4 percent higher on student effort, 6.1 percent higher on Academic Challenge, 10.8 percent higher on Student-Faculty Interaction, and 4.5 percent higher on Student Support.

We were able to also show in the study that, over a three-year period, service-learners had a higher course success rate (89 percent out of a total of 1,031 grades granted) than non-service-learners (65 percent out of 2,729 grades given). Even though the service-learners in general were more successful students (with a pre- service-learning semester overall success rate of 86.9 percent, compared with 73 percent for non-service-learners), they maintained their success in subsequent service-learning semesters while non-service-learners had a decrease in their success rates. For service-learners in developmental courses, course success rates, across three semesters were 80 percent, compared to 58.4 percent for non-service-learners. The three-semester next semester re-enrollment rate of service-learners was 76.1 percent, compared to 61.0 percent for non-service-learners. Service-learners also had higher graduation/transfer rates (13.1 percent) than non-service-learners (10.5 percent).

Evolution of Kapi'olani Service and Sustainability Learning (KSSL)

With these assessment results in hand, we began the development of a new Civic Action Plan in 2016, supported with funding from Campus Compact and the AAC&U Theory to Practice initiative. And with inspired and emboldened faculty leadership within the College's Faculty Senate Sustainability Standing Committee, as well as student and faculty energy within the broader UH system, the campus was able to expand its service-learning emphasis to include Sustainability and Climate Action Education.

In the College's current Strategic Plan, there are two specific performance measures that the Service and Sustainability Learning program is tracking. The first measure is to increase the number of students completing service-learning assignments annually from 700 to 900, and the second measure is to increase the number of sustainability-designated courses from 27 to 60, and to develop "Pathways to UH 4-year campuses." Hypothetically, the two measures are designed to increase together and reinforce each other. The first measure (service-learner increases) is in the "Engagement" and "Learning" phases of our Student Success Model, while the second measure (sustainability-designated course increase and transfer pathway) is in the "Learning" and "Achievement" phase of this model, which align with the KELA model.

In 2017-18, 898 students completed service-learning timesheets. Half of these students served in our Environmental Service-Learning Pathway, followed by service-learning student engagement in the Health, Education, Bridging Generations, Intercultural Education, and Arts, History and Culture Pathways. Forty-one sustainability-designated course sections have been developed, and they have been integrated across the general education curriculum into an "Academic Subject Certificate in Sustainability" within the Associate of Arts degree. Ten students completed this certificate and degree in spring 2019.

Since IIE and IIF are both included in the "Learning" phase of our Student Success Model, which is linked to our Strategic Plan, the remainder of this chapter will focus on the learning outcomes assessment innovations we have implemented since 2014.

KSSL Reflection Assessment

Each semester at the College, about 200 students participate in service-learning projects in about 30 courses, ranging from Anthropology to Second Language Teaching. The majority are first-year students from language, natural science and social science courses and major in liberal arts and sciences fields, such as natural sciences, and various CTE fields, such as occupational therapy. In order to complete their projects, students must submit a time sheet with at least 20 hours, an evaluation from their supervisor, and a written reflection about their service. Here is the prompt, which aligns with the College's general education SLOs.

As Hill et al. 2004 write, prompt A is "related to critical thinking skills that evaluate whether students are able to identify and describe the social problem and articulate how they contributed to the solution" (176). Prompt B is about "academic development" and "asks students to articulate how they applied course knowledge to solve real-world problems" (176) Prompts C and D, developed as part of a grant from the Teagle Foundation (see more below), seeks to engage students in reflection on their "commitments for civic and moral responsibility." Prompt D also focuses on students' "personal insights and transformation" (176).

Table 11.1: Kapi'olani's General Education Student Learning Outcomes

A.	Statement of the Problem: Identify the societal or ecological problem you have helped to address through your service. Explain how you have helped.
B.	Learning: Discuss at least 3 concepts/theories from your coursework that have helped you do your service. Describe experience during your service that have helped you understand those concepts/theories.
C.	Civic Context: As an informed individual and citizen, discuss the issue you explained above as a public or community problem. What elements of unfairness or injustice does the problem have? Do you believe more people should care about the problem? Why or why not? Discuss one or more solutions to the problem.
D.	Goals: Explain how your coursework and service activities have shaped your personal, academic, or professional goals. From the list below, select all the ones you are interested in doing and discuss at least one goal in detail. Explain how the action(s) you will take will help reduce the impact of the problem. 1. Support family, friends, and/or neighbors who are affected by the problem. 2. Serve, or fundraise to support, a community-based organization that is working on the problem. 3. Patronize businesses that are actively working to lessen the severity of the problem or are committed to not making the problem worse. 4. Convene a dialogue with policy-makers who are working on the problem. 5. Advocate with public officials and/or legislators who are working on the problem. 6. Start, lead, or join a campus group that is working on the problem. 7. Take another course to gain a new perspective on the problem. 8. Complete a degree that will provide me with the knowledge, skills, and attitudes to work on the problem in my profession. 9. Other (specify)

In order to assess the reflections, we developed a rubric based on the AACU's VALUE rubrics as well as Gail Lynn Goldberg's "Revising an Engineering Design Rubric: A Case Study Illustrating Principles and

Practices to Ensure Technical Quality of Rubrics." (https://pareonline. net/getvn.asp?v=19&n=8)

To prepare the assessment, the Service-Learning coordinator set up a Laulima (UH system's content management system) website for essay collection. Service-learning faculty determined that assessing 30 essays per semester was satisfactory as long as they were chosen randomly. The 30 essays (out of about 300) are chosen using a random number generator. They are downloaded from Laulima and printed in hard copy. They are numbered 1-30. For each essay, the student's name is blacked out, missing page numbers are written in, and every fifth line are marked so important moments could be referenced more easily.

The essays are assessed using the following protocol:

1. Eight readers are split into four groups. Each group focuses on one of the four rubric questions (A, B, C or D).
2. The 30 essays are divided among the four groups in roughly even batches (8, 7, 8 and 7, respectively).
3. The readers of a particular group read each essay in their batch and determine the score for their assigned question. Each reader records his/her scores on his/her individual rating sheet (0-4, 4 highest). Each reader also notes the line numbers of evidence for the score and "aha!" moments (which may be used in assessment/promotional materials) on his/her individual rating sheet.
4. After the readers in a particular group finish scoring their batch of essays, they share scores. They discuss divergent scores and agree upon a score. Only whole numbers are permitted. If the readers cannot agree, the lower score is taken.
5. After members of a group settle on a score for each essay in a batch, they record their agreed-upon scores on a master sheet for their assigned question.
6. After members of a group finishes a batch of essays, they give the batch to the next group in this order: A-B, B-C, C-D, D-A. Each group receives another batch from another group.
7. The scoring continues in this way until each group finishes all 30 essays.
8. After the scoring is done, each group's master score sheet and each reader's individual score sheet are submitted to the faculty coordinator.

Results

The target on the four-point scale is 2, which is what we think a sophomore in college should score. The double readers asessment value generated discussion about what might be done to improve the scores. For example, a common theme every semester is asking faculty to integrate the reflection component into their grading rather than just considering it as extra credit, as many faculty do. The assessment process resulted in changes to orientation and mid-term reflection workshops as well as the creation of a new journal. In addition it motivated us to ask our community partners to more explicitly discuss with our students the societal or ecological problems they seek to remedy.

From 2013-2016, the College, along with the Community College National Center for Community Engagement, led a Teagle Foundation multi-campus grant focused on a single Big Question. The question was: "How do we build our commitment to moral and civic responsibility for diverse, equitable, healthy and sustainable communities?" The last two iterations of this assessment method were developed with these Teagle Foundation funds and can be further examined at https://teachingtobigquestions.wordpress.com/.

The next iteration will have similar prompts, perhaps more generally or simply articulated. It will also allow for different artifacts, those that better match our students' disciplines, course levels, and backgrounds. About 2/3 of our students are taking a science or language (Chinese, Japanese or Korean) class in which substantial writing or writing in English is not a major component. These classes do not require first-year composition as a pre-requisite. Further, about a third of our students are international, and up to half speak English as a second language. It seems too much to ask the majority of our students to produce a high-quality (English-language) essay that their current class or prior classes/experiences have not necessarily prepared them to write. Some possible future artifacts could include: a lower-stakes or developmental writing assignment, such as one an electronic portfolio could accommodate; a poster presentation, slide deck or Prezi with transcript; or an audio/visual piece, such as a podcast or video. The future also asks us to address institutional learning outcomes, develop a new set of general education SLOs, and the reflection as an assessment for course SLOs.

The Kapiʻolani Research Scholars Project: Assessing Sustainability Outcomes

In Fall 2019, the college launched an Academic Subject Certificate in Sustainability. This 14-credit micro-credential is embedded in general education – no additional credits, no new courses. A Sustainability marker is affixed to sections with a "primary and specific emphasis" on sustainability, using criteria that are linked to AASHE STARS, and further developed by a systemwide advisory council. Individual course sections can carry this marker and be counted towards the certificate. The benefit for the college is in recruiting and engagement; the benefit for students is in curricular coherence and being part of a smaller cohort of sustainability-focused classes.

The campus Sustainability and Climate Action Plan for 2016-2021 (to be reviewed and renewed with the new campus Strategic Plan in 2021) is driven by a UH System Executive Level Policy on Sustainability, which states that the college will develop "new courses and programs related to sustainability" and also supports "the integration of sustainability principles into existing curricula where appropriate."

After conducting an inventory of courses and building this to 13 faculty teaching 28 course sections with a sustainability focus, sustainability faculty were ready to define a certificate. The next step of the process was to consider how to assess the certificate as a program, and how to define and assess student learning outcomes for sustainability. The Kapiʻolani Research Scholars Program offered $1,000 stipends to faculty who agreed to work in teams to address weak areas in assessment, and this incentive was enough to bring together five faculty from English, Economics, Pacific Island Studies, Botany, and Biology. Additional faculty participated as ad hoc members.

The group designed a year-long study to pilot three assessment tools. The study had six research questions:

1. What is the impact of sustainability-focused (S-focused) courses on students' sustainability mindset (measured by self-reported values and attitudes toward sustainability)?
2. What is the impact of S-focused courses on students' knowledge of core concepts of sustainability (measured by faculty evaluation of a sample of papers/projects/presentations as well as student performance on the Sulitest)?
3. What is the impact of S-focused courses on students' interest in a sustainability-related academic major or occupation (measured by

self-reported interest in the SALG)?
4. Is there a dosage effect of S-focused courses on the outcomes in (1), (2), or (3)? [i.e., Are the impacts of S-focused courses stronger among students who have taken more than one S-focused course?]
5. Is there a population effect of S-focused courses on the outcomes in (1), (2), or (c)?

Target populations of the study:

- Early college students (on-site high school sections)
- International students (ESOL sections)
- Distance education students (online sections)
- 1st year (< 30 credits) and 2nd year (30+ credits) students (F2F sections)

A key question was whether S-focused courses contribute to greater student achievement (measured by successful course completion in S-focused sections) compared to non-S-focused sections.

The data collection instruments were:

1. Student Assessment of Learning Gains (SALG) Survey instrument that focuses on the degree to which specific course aspects have enabled student learning. See http://www.salgsite.org/about for detailed description.
2. Sulitest: A summative assessment tool developed in multiple languages to assess literacy in core sustainability dimensions. See http://www.sulitest.org/en/test-certificate.html for detailed description.
3. Faculty evaluation of students' paper/project/presentation using an adapted Wiek rubric (see discussion below).
4. Course completion data at the end of the semester.

The research team held weekly meetings, an IRB approval was submitted, and participating faculty agreed to build the assessment tools into their Spring 2018 courses. Students took the SALG pre-test within the first two weeks of classes and the Sulitest as part of a course exam or activity. After completing a paper or project related to sustainability, they were asked to reflect on their learning via the SALG post-test within the last two weeks of the semester.

These assessments were used in 16 course sections with 259 students. 68% of those students indicated it was their first Sustainability Focused course and they already had a decided major.

Results

The SALG posttest revealed that some concepts of sustainability are taught across more sections than others: for example, sustainable materials management (waste management) and social justice and equity showed lower self-reported learning, while ecological footprint and Local First showed high learning gains. The most interesting insight from the SALG was that at the beginning of the semester only 36.9% were interested in a major related to sustainability; by the end of the semester, that number rose to 69.8%. Sustainability focused courses increased student interest in sustainability.

From the Sulitest, we learned that students have very individualized profiles of sustainability literacy. For example, one student scored a zero on "systemic change" and another aced that section but had a much lower understanding of "human-constructed systems." In other words, coursework builds on an inconsistent sustainability knowledge base.

Some specific Sulitest findings were that 53% of students could recognize the Brundtland definition of Sustainability, and 40% could define "fair trade". However, only 28% knew the goals of "the Paris Agreement". These are component vocabularies of sustainability

Lastly, the assessment tool that was the most fun for the research team was designing a rubric to assess a variety of course projects (papers, presentations, websites). Wiek et al. (2011) developed a rubric for assessing Key Competencies in Sustainability: Systems thinking, Futures thinking, Values thinking, Strategic thinking, and Collaboration. Working from this rubric, the team found that to assess first-year community college students, a "pre-novice" level would have to be defined. This stimulated discussion about foundational knowledge, skills, and attitudes.

The results of the difficult, but stimulating half-day of project scoring resulted in some significant insights:

- Students did well in "connecting decision making to consequences", with 57% of the sample actually achieving Novice level on the Wiek et al. rubric.
- Students were "approaching novice" in three areas: define a problem (67%), identify an intervention point (76%), and visualize the timescale of their own life (76%).

Opportunities for program improvement were discerned as well:

- "explain how elements are connected across domains" (57% did NOT achieve pre-novice)
- "Identify injustice in sustainability" (76% did NOT achieve pre-novice)

Reflecting on the experience of practitioner research for assessment, the project (and the idea of a stipend) incentivized faculty to make time for meetings that they enjoyed and valued. The questions stimulated their genuine interest and desire to learn more about effective pedagogies for teaching sustainability as well as learning new sustainability content from each other. The goal is to continue to integrate the assessment tools into Sustainability courses at least one semester per year.

Not all of the research questions or project goals were achieved. Data on course completion was difficult to obtain due to student identification numbers (surprising, since that seemed to be the easiest data point.) IRB approval process placed an undue burden on one team member—supporting this institutionally seems reasonable. Due to a technicality with the IRB, the stipends have not yet been awarded. However, the interest and accolades from peers and campus leadership provided visibility to the hard work of faculty teaching sustainability-related content and allowed the team to flex their research muscles to approach assessment with genuine curiosity and a desire to improve.

Conclusion

As the College continues to improve the depth and quality of its assessment strategies, it remains engaged with national organizations focused on service-learning and civic and community engagement (Campus Compact), science and civic engagement (Center for Science and Civic Engagement/SUNY Stony Brook), sustainability education (Association for Advancement of Sustainability in Higher Education), and environmental science and policy (National Council for Science and the Environment). In addition, the College's past engagement with the Teagle Foundation and new engagement with the Keck Foundation on "Transcending Barriers to Success: Connecting Indigenous and Western Knowledge Systems to Tackle Climate Change" are continuing to sharpen our focus to strengthen social and environmental justice locally, regionally, nationally and globally. This focus has emerged not just as a big question but as THE BIG QUESTION for students now and through the decade of the 2020s and beyond.

In the 2019-2020 academic year, we will be working to further develop and assess both our Civic Action and Sustainability and Climate Action Plans and carry this dialogue into campus Strategic Planning for 2021-2026. We intend to have our students more fully engage in moral and civic responsibility for diverse, equitable, healthy and sustainable communities for themselves and their families, and to more fully develop their capacities as responsible members of their communities while rethinking and retracting from the consumerism that is engulfing them.

Works Cited

Bailey, T., Jaggars, S. S., & Jenkins, D. (2015, March). What we know about guided pathways. *Community College Research Center*. New York, NY: Teachers College, Columbia University. Retreived from http://ccrc.tc.columbia.edu/publications/what-we-know-about-guided-pathways-packet.html

Goldberg, G. L. (2014). Revising an engineering design rubric: A case study illustrating principles and practices to ensure technical quality of rubrics." *Practical Assessment, Research, and Evaluation*, 19, Article 8. koi.org/10.7275/vq7m-e490

Hill, Y. Z., Renner, T., Acoba, F., Hiser, K., & Franco, R. W. (2014). Service-learning's role in achieving institutional outcomes: Engagement, learning, and achievement. A. Traver & Z. Katz (Eds.), *Service-learning at the American community college* (pp. 169-182). New York, NY: Palgrave Macmillan.

Lewallen, W. (2019). External evaluation report. *Kapi'olani Community College*. Retrieved from: www.kapiolani.hawaii.edu/wp-content/uploads/2019/01/Kapiolani_EER_2018.pdf.

AFTERWORD

As the essays in this volume make clear, there is a robust movement for civic education and civic and community engagement in America's community colleges. Rooted in a long tradition of community service-learning, this work now includes policy debate and engagement, mobilizing for local community development, and preparing for the duties of civic life beyond college.

This is a proud account of work in a wide range of colleges, urban and rural, large and small, all dedicated to the idea that post-secondary education is not narrow preparation for the labor market, and that the skills of citizenship (for citizens and non-citizens alike) are among the outcomes we ought to expect from community colleges.

However, you'd be hard-pressed to know this if you reviewed the publications, conference announcements, funding opportunities, and "strategic priorities" of national community college organizations, college systems, and foundations. With rare exceptions—like Campus Compact's "Community Colleges for Democracy"—the idea that a community college education must include an engagement with the practical arts of democracy is nowhere to be found.

This is partly a legacy of the dominant narrative about community colleges: that they serve to prepare men and women for the job market, or prepare them for transfer to universities. And one could argue that there are priorities enough in the current focus on increasing access to higher education, establishing programs that provide equity to those historically marginalized, or greater completion and success rates for all. These are powerful and important projects, and it is welcome that legislatures and foundations and college system emphasize them.

But none of these priorities ought to eclipse the civic mission of our colleges, and none of them explain the relative silence on civic outcomes in our national associations and state systems. Put simply, there is a yawning gap between the sophisticated work detailed in this book and the national conversations about post-secondary education, access and success, equity, and cost. That gap would be acceptable if civic work happened anyway, under the radar, and the programs detailed in this volume were the norm in colleges across the land. But that is not the case, and hundreds of thousands, indeed millions, of community college students never have the opportunities described here.

Students themselves want more. Every single account in this book shows the enthusiasm and passion with which students embrace this work, and learn about themselves, others with whom they disagree, and how policy and power work. And, as the work at Piedmont Virginia shows, students can engage the most difficult and contentious issues of race and violence with care and clarity.

Students are right to want more. And the faculty, staff, and administrators in our colleges who want to emphasize civic work will have to confront their aversion to politics, their fear of being called partisan, their anxiety about funding and governing boards and community reaction, if this work is serious.

Finally, we who have built these programs and are legitimately proud of their success, have to ask ourselves another question. Are these programs enough to prepare students to address the three largest issues faced by young people, particularly students from low-income communities: the crisis in American democracy, inequality, and the climate crisis?

By the time this book appears, a president will have been impeached but not convicted. A country will remain deeply divided over the most fundamental aspects of a constitutional regime. When only a third of American adults can name a branch of government or define the separation of powers, when 48% of registered Republicans think the separation of powers is an annoying hindrance of presidential prerogative, and a third of Americans think a military regime is acceptable, what role do colleges play in the defense of democracy? Or, has it become partisan to defend democracy? Are civic and community engagement programs adequate to prepare students? What would a national campaign for civic and democratic learning have to confront and overcome?

On the issue of inequality—the enduring and defining element of the lives of most community college students—do we continue to teach a modified form of market fundamentalism where persons craft their own futures through hard work and grit? Or, do we learn from the many and multiple analyses of contemporary capitalism that social outcomes are also driven by policy and politics—and students can affect their lives through collective and public work as much as they can through individual striving?

On the climate front, do we adequately prepare students for the deep and wrenching policy and political choices they will face over the next fifteen years of their adulthood? How do our civic and community engagement programs develop the critical skills and understandings required to face the climate crisis? Or, what can colleges learn from their civic and community engagement programs to develop a college-wide commitment to climate science and an understanding of the full dimensions of the climate disaster?

Again, what stops us? Why isn't a preparation for climate disaster part of our civic mission? Has it become partisan to tell the truth about climate science or insist that an adequate civic education now must include the climate crisis? If it's partisan to insist that students understand the difference between 1.5 and 3 degrees Celsius, or the policy options to liberate our economy from fossil fuels and our agriculture from over-grazing, in what sense have we provided students an education to the dominant civic issues of our time?

The essays in this book suggest that colleges know how to build engaging programs on civic issues. How to make them the norm and make them the models for confronting the dominant issues of our time is another matter altogether. One suspects that the students will force the issue.

Brian Murphy
President Emeritus, De Anza College

EDITORS AND CONTRIBUTORS

Editors

Verdis L. Robinson, *Community College Civic Engagement Specialist*

Verdis L. Robinson served as the inaugural director for community college engagement at Campus Compact. As a crusader of community college civic education, Robinson helped to create Campus Compact's Community Colleges for Democracy (CC4D) network as part of his portfolio after serving as a tenured assistant professor of history and African-American studies at Monroe Community College (MCC) in Rochester, NY. Additionally, Robinson served as the national director of The Democracy Commitment, a national initiative for advancing civic engagement in community colleges.

Clayton Hurd, *Director of Professional Learning,* Campus Compact

Dr. Clayton Hurd received his Ph.D. in cultural anthropology from the University of California, Santa Cruz. Before arriving at Campus Compact in 2018, Hurd held the dual role at Stanford University as lecturer in the Program on Urban Studies and senior program director of public service research and graduate student engagement in the Haas Center for Public Service. Previous to that, he held dual appointments as assistant professor of anthropology and director of the Center for Service-Learning at the College of Coastal Georgia, and assistant professor of education and director of the Office of Service-Learning at Colorado State University.

Contributors

Francisco Acoba, *Associate Professor of English*, Kapi'olani Community College, HI

Francisco Acoba teaches literature and writing (with a sustainability focus) and also helps run the college's Service and Sutainability Learning Program.

Sarah Diel-Hunt, *Vice President of Enrollment and Student Services,* Heartland Community College, IL

Dr. Sarah Diel-Hunt serves as vice president of enrollment and student services at Heartland Community College where she has worked to establish curricular and co-curricular efforts in civic engagement and service-learning.

Dr. Robert Franco, *Director, Institutional Effectiveness and Professor, Pacific Anthropology,* Kapi'olani Community College, HI

For 35 years, Dr. Franco has been an ecological and demographic anthropologist focusing on contemporary Hawaiian, Samoan, and Pacific Islander educational, employment, health, environmental, climate and cultural issues. Since 2000, he has been director of planning and grants and institutional effectiveness at Kapi'olani Community College, the second-largest college in the ten campus University of Hawai'i system. He oversees the Kapi'olani Service and Sustainability Learning program. He is a senior faculty fellow for Campus Compact (compact.org), leadership fellow for the NSF program, Science Education for Civic Engagements and Responsibilities (SENCER) and SENCER Hawai'i, and current chair of the NCSE Community College Network (formerly CCASE).

Editors and Contributors

Krista Hiser, *Professor of English, Director, Center for Sustainability Across Curriculum,* Kapi'olani Community College, HI

Krista Hiser is a community college professor of English and also serves as the director of sustainability across curriculum for the University of Hawaii ten campus system. She has also published on community engagement, service-learning, organizational change, post-apocalyptic and cli-fi literature. She is senior fellow for community colleges at the National Council for Science & the Environment.

Stephen K. Hunt, *Professor of Communication, Executive Director of the School of Communication,* Illinois State University, IL

Dr. Stephen Hunt serves as professor of communication and executive director of the School of Communication at Illinois State University. He recently completed an assignment serving as co-chair of Illinois State's American Democracy Project. As an American Association of State Colleges and Universities (AASCU) civic fellow for political engagement, he helps lead national efforts to sharpen the political and civic leadership skills of today's college students.

Lena Jones, *Political Science Faculty,* Minneapolis College, MN

Lena Jones (MA, Political Science; MS, Experiential Education) is a political science faculty member and the faculty coordinator of the Community Development A.S. Degree Program at Minneapolis College. Lena has been involved with many civic engagement initiatives during her time at Minneapolis College and in 2013, she received a two-year fellowship from the Bush Foundation to explore ways to build equitable and reciprocal higher education/community partnerships. Lena is also the Minnesota and Mississippi coordinator of Community Learning Partnership (CLP), a national organization that builds partnerships between higher education institutions, community organizations, and governments to create educational pathways into community change careers.

Connie Jorgensen, *Assistant Professor of Political Science, Civic Engagement Coordinator,* Piedmont Virginia Community College, VA

Connie teaches political science at Piedmont Virginia Community College where she also coordinates civic engagement activities. She also leads the planning team for the colleges' new Quality Enhancement Plan on Civic Engagement.

Lisa Lawrason, PhD, *Professor of Political Science,* Delta College, MI

Lisa Lawrason, PhD, is a professor of political science at Delta College, where she has taught American politics and constitutional issues courses for 13 years. Both inside and outside the classroom, she devotes her efforts to politically empowering community college students, inviting them to engage in the civic lives of their community and providing opportunities to do so. As the co-campus coordinator of The Democracy Commitment, her efforts have defined Delta College as a national leader in civic learning.

Lori Moog, *Director of Service-learning and Community Outreach,* Raritan Valley Community College, NJ

Ms. Lori Moog is the director of service-learning and community Outreach at Raritan Valley Community College. She has coordinated the program since 1996, helping it to earn national awards including the President's Higher Education Community Service Honor Roll annually since 2006, the Carnegie Community Engagement Classification in 2008 and Reclassification in 2015, and the 2018 New Jersey State Governor's Jefferson Award for students' extraordinary volunteer service to the community. Ms. Moog has offered more than 60 professional development workshops to college faculty and administrators on developing service-learning programs regionally, nationally, and internationally. She has extensive experience in developing and coordinating campus and community programs.

Erin Riney, *Director of Student Engagement,* Durham Technical Community College, NC

Erin Riney is the director of student engagement at Durham Technical Community College in Durham, North Carolina. She championed and developed service-learning at Durham Tech, founded the college's food pantry, and established and directed the college's first community engagement office. Her other professional interests include voter engagement, supporting under-resourced students, and teaching first-year experience courses.

Patty D. Robinson, *Faculty Director of Civic and Community Engagement,* College of the Canyons, CA

Patty has worked at College of the Canyons since 1999 and has served in various roles, including sociology professor, Sociology Department chair, and dean of the Social Sciences and Business Division. She holds a Ph.D. in sociology from the University of California, Davis, where she pursued her interests in women's history and medical sociology and eventually focused on the rise of 19th and 20th Century women's organizations. Inspired by *A Crucible Moment* (2012) and longing to return to her "sociological roots," she currently spearheads the College's campus-wide emphasis on civic, community, and political engagement as faculty director, civic and community engagement initiatives.

John Saltmarsh, *Professor of Higher Education in the Department of Leadership in Education in the College of Education and Human Development*, University of Massachusetts, Boston

John is professor of higher education in the Department of Leadership in Education in the College of Education and Human Development at the University of Massachusetts, Boston. John publishes widely on community-engaged teaching, learning, and research, and organizational change in higher education. A sampling of his co-edited books includes *The Elective Carnegie Community Engagement Classification: Constructing a Successful Application for First-Time and Re-Classification Applicants* (2017), *Publicly Engaged Scholars: Next Generation Engagement and the Future of Higher Education* (2016), and *To Serve a Larger Purpose: Engagement for Democracy and the Transformation of Higher Education (2011)*. He is the co-author of the *Democratic Engagement White Paper* (NERCHE, 2009) and *Full Participation: Building the Architecture for Diversity and Public Engagement in Higher Education* (2011).

Emilie Stander, *Associate Professor of Environmental Science* , Raritan Valley Community College, NJ

Dr. Emilie Stander is an ecosystem ecologist and associate professor of environmental science at Raritan Valley Community College (RVCC) in Branchburg, NJ, where she teaches courses such as Ecology, Environmental Science and Sustainability, Ecology Experience Abroad, and Applied Research in Environmental Science. Emilie is the director of RVCC's Water Quality Laboratory and co-director of RVCC's Center for Environmental Studies, both of which provide platforms for student and community engagement in environmental monitoring, research, and sustainability projects. Emilie received her Bachelor's of Science in environmental science from Brown University and her PhD in Ecology and Evolution from Rutgers University.

Editors and Contributors

John J. Theil, *Professor of Political Science & Director of the Center for Civic Engagement,* Lone Star College – Kingwood, TX

Dr. John J. Theis is the Director of the Center for Civic Engagement for the Lone Star College – Kingwood and a professor of political science. He also serves as a member of the Board of Directors for the National Issues Forum Institute. He has been involved in civic engagement work for over 20 years, started the LSC-Kingwood Public Achievement program in 2010, and was one of the founders of the Kingwood College Center for Civic Engagement. Dr. Theis holds his Ph.D. from the University of Arizona.